# Living Rooms

## Interior Decoration in Wales 400–1960

Charles Kightly

**Cadw**

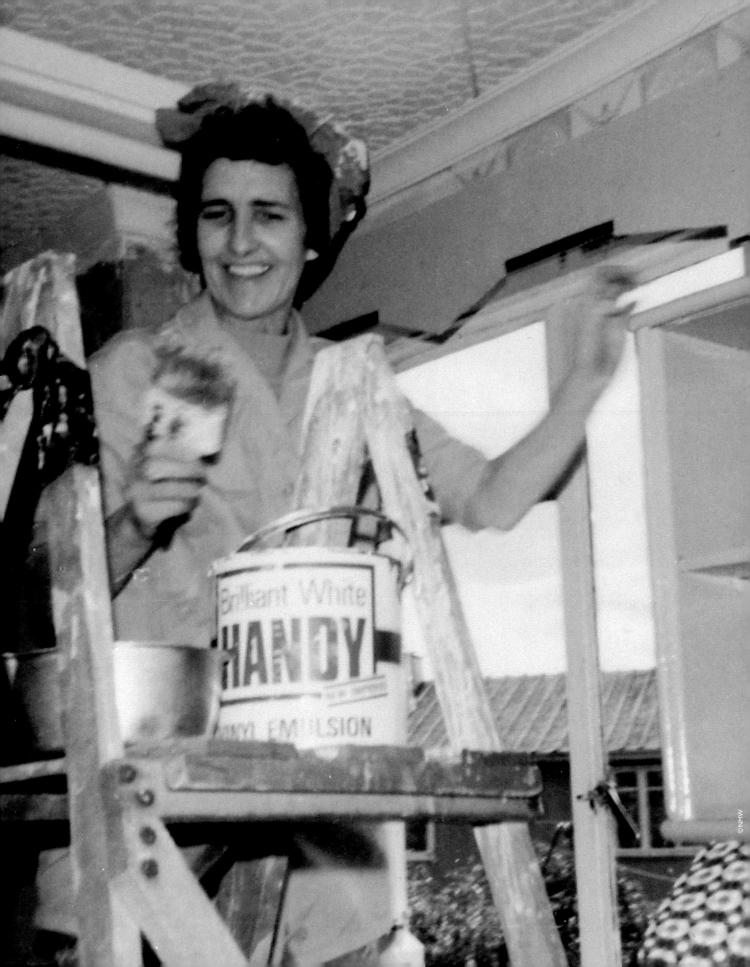

# An Introduction to Living Rooms in Wales

In recent years, public interest in interior decoration has grown almost to a fever pitch: but a preoccupation with the embellishment of our domestic surroundings is nothing new. This book seeks to provide an overview (space will allow no more) of how people in Wales decorated their house interiors over a period of more than a thousand years, from the emergence of Wales as a distinct entity until the Plastics Age of the 1960s.

This is an ambitious scheme and, to render it feasible, strict limitations have been set. So this is neither a history book, nor a book about Welsh culture, house architecture, house building, or house types. It surveys domestic interiors in dwellings from cottages to stately homes and castles, but excludes monasteries, churches and even household chapels. It concentrates moreover on the decoration of living rooms — rooms where people ate, slept, and entertained their guests — rather than service rooms like kitchens and workshops, or facilities like bathrooms and toilets. Movable furniture — with the notable exception of wall hangings and similar decorative features — has regretfully been excluded.

Another limitation, imposed by lack of information rather than lack of space, is that the house interiors of the wealthy (and in later periods of the 'middling sort') are more comprehensively covered than those of the poor, about which very little is known until recent times. The disproportionate survival of high-status decorative features like tapestries, and the almost total disappearance of more modest and once far more widespread cheaper materials, also skew the picture. The house interiors of ordinary people, and everyday decorative materials — all the more valuable and fascinating because of their rare survival — have therefore been highlighted whenever possible. The rooms of a post-war prefab with lino and wallpaper are just as important a historic interior as the silk-hung chambers of a Georgian mansion.

This book strives to dispel the misconception that the people of pre-industrial Wales lived either in stark fortresses or filthy hovels, both alike devoid of comfort, colour and decoration. This notion, still assiduously promoted by films, television and novels, is inadvertently reinforced by the presentation of many older dwellings in Wales with bare stone walls, exposed timber framing and — where it exists

at all — battered and time-blackened furniture. At Plas Mawr, Conwy, Cadw has pioneered the historically accurate and less misleading re-creation of rooms with their original vibrant colours.

This book provides a comprehensive background of evidence and illustration for such a re-creation. It is divided into four chronological sections. Each includes a short historical summary of the relevant period, particularly as it affected changes to interiors; a note on how we know about such changes; and features on new types or uses of rooms, new fashions in decoration, and newly available decorative materials. Photographic 'swatches' illustrating these materials are featured inside the cover flaps.

Finally, although nearly all the interiors illustrated are in Wales, not all are exclusively 'Welsh' interiors. Many, especially in greater houses and in later periods, followed widespread trends prevalent throughout Britain and indeed Europe: no border has ever been able to seal out fashion. A thread of distinctively Welsh interior decoration, increasingly embattled but surviving to this day, can nevertheless be traced through the ten centuries and more covered by this survey.

Armed with a tin of *Handy* vinyl emulsion paint — a revolutionary post-war material — Mrs Anne Jones prepares to decorate the ceiling of her kitchen at 24, Brodawel, Merthyr Tydfil, in 1952 (left).

# Earliest Interiors
## 400–1400

# Setting the scene: household interiors in Wales before 1400

The millennium between 400 and 1400 saw first the emergence of Christian Welsh princedoms from the wreck of the Roman empire, despite encroachment by Anglo-Saxons and raids by Vikings. Then, after 1066, came the ebb and flow of Norman invasions and Welsh counter-attacks; the brief flowering of a unified Welsh realm under Llywelyn ap Gruffudd (the Last); and after 1282 its conquest by Edward I of England. There followed a period of comparatively peaceful coexistence during the fourteenth century.

To describe how the interiors of living rooms in Wales were decorated during these many troubled centuries is a difficult task, for no room interiors survive in anything like their complete form until the very end of the period, and then often only as roofless, and always bare-walled, shells. Indeed it is probable that no ordinary Welsh domestic buildings at all survive from this period, and certainly no timber-framed house in Wales has been tree-ring dated to earlier than the beginning of the fifteenth century. The precious few surviving traces of domestic interior decoration from the period all come from stone-built castles or bishops' palaces. Until recent times, we know much more about the interiors of the rich and powerful than those of the 'middling sort', and still less about those of the poor.

We must look to archaeology, documentary records, and a few contemporary descriptions for information about early interior decoration. Archaeological research is producing intriguing evidence of domestic life in the *llysoedd* (courts) of the early Welsh princes. Sixth- and seventh-century sites like the hillfort at Dinas Powys, near Cardiff, and the unique crannog, or artificial island, in Llangorse Lake, Powys, a ninth-century residence of the Welsh kings of Brycheiniog, have yielded traces of comparatively luxurious lifestyles there. Archaeological sites like Rhosyr on Anglesey, a thirteenth-century *llys* of Llywelyn ab Iorwerth (the Great) of Gwynedd, provide a valuable backdrop to the few contemporary documents which describe, if not how homes were decorated, then at least how they were lived in.

Of these documents perhaps the most revealing are the laws of Hywel Dda. The earliest surviving manuscripts date from the thirteenth century, but the laws may refer back to considerably earlier traditions. By recording such matters as the duties of household officials and the value of domestic furnishings, these laws provide invaluable hints about the appearance of living rooms. So too do the observations of that tireless writer and traveller, Gerald of Wales, made during his famous journey through the land in 1188.

Yet more hints can be gleaned from a variety of other sources, ranging from the matter-of-fact financial accounts of the officials responsible for furnishing Edward I's castles to passages in the *Mabinogion*, Welsh tales written down by the thirteenth century but perhaps based on much older oral traditions. Descriptions of interiors by bards like the fourteenth-century poets, Iolo Goch and Dafydd ap Gwilym — though strongly coloured by both poetic licence and the need to flatter the patrons on whom the writers' livelihoods depended — also demonstrate vividly that better-off Welshmen did not occupy the stark and comfortless dwellings so often depicted by the modern media.

©NMW

©NMW

Evidence for a luxurious lifestyle in fifth- to seventh-century Dinas Powys (top) includes wine jars from North Africa and the Mediterranean, tableware from France, glass drinking bowls, ornamental metalwork and jewellery.

The pattern on an intricately woven ninth-century textile (above), found near the Llangorse Lake 'royal island', has been reconstructed. Decorated with bird and lion motifs, it was apparently part of a woman's dress, but similar textiles might well have been used for wall hangings.

Bedclothes and bed-curtains added colour as well as warmth and comfort to medieval interiors — and also a degree of privacy from servants. This early fourteenth-century manuscript (left) reputedly depicts Gerald of Wales's glamorous grandmother Princess Nest, in bed with one of her many lovers, King Henry I of England.

Illustrations in a thirteenth-century copy manuscript of the laws of Hywel Dda (below) show two of the officials responsible for the efficiency and comfort of a princely household. On the left is the *penteulu*, or head of the household, in his ornamental chair, and on the right is the steward with a serving dish.

© National Library of Wales, Peniarth Ms. 28. f. 5r

© National Library of Wales, Peniarth Ms. 28. f. 3r

© Cambrian Archaeological Association

©NMW

Exaggerating (as he so often did), Gerald of Wales declared that 'the Welsh do not live in towns, villages or castles, but lead an almost solitary life in woodlands. There they do not raise great palaces, nor expensive and luxurious buildings of stone and mortar, but instead make do with houses of interwoven wattles, easily and cheaply built but adequate for a year or two.' This old house near Strata Florida, Ceredigion (above), which was ruinous when drawn in 1888 and has now vanished, may have been a more substantial descendant of the buildings he describes. Alternatively, Gerald may have been describing a *hafod*, or temporary summer dwelling. Its descendant was the *tŷ un nos*, a house raised during a single night to establish squatters' rights. This experimental *tŷ un nos* (left) was built at St Fagans National History Museum, near Cardiff, using rough timbers tied together and turves to cover the walls and roof. In any event — as Gerald knew perfectly well — the Welsh were building both permanent timber halls and stone castles by the time of his journey in 1188.

*'Fair timber house on a green mound ... with eight bright lofts where poets sleep ... nine halls (rooms), with a wardrobe in each ... like fine shops with beautiful contents, like well-stocked shops in London's Cheapside ... a tiled roof on every building, and a chimney that did not suffer smoke ... fair limewashed walls and fine glass windows like a church ...'*

*Iolo Goch's praise of Owain Glyn Dŵr's mansion at Sycharth, written in about 1390.*

# Halls, hearths and sleeping places

From the earliest to almost the latest records of interiors in Wales, three features stand out as essential — the hall or main living room; the hearth which warmed the house; and, in all but the earliest or humblest dwellings, a separate (or at least divided-off) sleeping place.

## The Hall

Until the seventeenth century — and in humbler dwellings much later — the hall was the principal room in any house, where nearly all the social activities of the inhabitants took place. Early documents indeed often use the word 'hall' as a synonym for the whole dwelling, even when it was only one of the many buildings which together made up a royal *llys*. The laws of Hywel Dda assumed that a princely hall would be at least partly constructed of timber, with its roof supported by six great wooden posts, which might be painted, carved and even gilded. It would also contain draught-excluding screens, and seating for greater and lesser folk, whose nearness to the king's throne was a precise indication of their status. The entire structure of early halls was indeed loaded with symbolism: it was surely as much for propaganda as for practical reasons that Edward I dismantled some of the timber-framed halls of the defeated Prince Llywelyn the Last and re-erected them within the stone castles and walled towns built to consolidate English rule. Of these the hall from Ystumgwern, re-erected at Harlech Castle, was surprisingly small — only some 18 feet (5.5m) wide by 37 feet (11.3m) long — but another, Llywelyn's Hall, built at Conwy but later moved to Caernarfon, was considerably larger.

©John Hodgson

An artist's impression shows the hall excavated at Rhosyr, near Newborough, Anglesey, as it may have appeared in the thirteenth century. One of the many halls of the independent Welsh princes of Gwynedd, this substantial building was apparently in use from before 1237 until the 1330s. It measured internally 55 feet (16.8m) long by 36 feet (11m) wide. It is shown as a timber-framed building, with a central hearth, a smoke louvre in its thatched roof, and cloth wall hangings: it is however possible that it had earth walls on stone footings. The attached stone building to the left may well have contained separate sleeping chambers.

©NMW

### The hearth

Whatever else the hall contained, its essential feature was a hearth or fireplace — a word whose Latin translation is *focus*. Until the very recent advent of central heating, a hearth was indeed the focus of every house. There a fire was kept burning both day and night: in early Welsh poems, 'a fireless hall' is a sad synonym for a house plundered or abandoned.

Set directly on the floor and usually near the centre of the room, the hearths of early halls had both advantages and disadvantages. A comparatively large number of people could sit around them; but the danger of accidental conflagration was considerable, and worst of all they could, and did, fill the hall with smoke, as surviving smoke-blackened roof timbers in late medieval and even Tudor halls testify. Most better-built early halls had rainproof louvres or other roof apertures to allow some smoke to escape, but until the nineteenth century some humble cottages survived which had only doors and windows as smoke exits for the floor hearth, so that in bad weather their inhabitants had to choose between being smoked or frozen.

Chris Jones-Jenkins for Cadw

The centrally placed floor hearth is undoubtedly the oldest and longest enduring type of fireplace. This example in the recreated Celtic house at St Fagans National History Museum (top) displays copies of elaborate Iron Age firedogs. Decorative fire irons remained important status symbols long after floor hearths had given way to more convenient wall fireplaces and chimneys.

Smokiness apart, another disadvantage of central hearths was that they could not easily be used to heat upper rooms with timber floors. In this reconstruction of the fourteenth-century first-floor hall at Dolforwyn Castle, near Newtown, Powys (above), however, this problem was ingeniously solved by building a stone pillar to support the hearth safely.

## The sleeping space

From either hearsay or perhaps personal experience, Gerald of Wales describes the inhabitants of a twelfth-century Welsh house cheerfully sleeping all together on a communal bed of rushes at one end of a hall, covered only by a coarse locally woven cloak-blanket called a *brychan*. Stories in the *Mabinogion* also mention beds made up within the hall, sometimes on a low platform to keep them clear of damp from the floor. The habit of raising beds on platforms persisted throughout the Middle Ages, even in great houses, and vestigial bed platforms were still being built into some Welsh houses in mid-Victorian times, if only as a matter of custom.

From other *Mabinogion* tales, however, and from the laws of Hywel Dda, it is clear that the owner and perhaps his wife had sleeping chambers separated from the hall, though they slept on pallet beds made up daily from straw or rushes, covered like Gerald's communal sleepers by the *brychan* which may well qualify as the earliest known Welsh 'furnishing fabric'. These early chambers were not private or exclusive. The king shared his with his chamberlain and other personal servants, and though the queen's male chamberlain was exiled for propriety to a bed by the privy, she shared her chamber with one or more maids, near enough to 'hear the slightest word the queen says.' The presence of servants in the bedchambers of the great, ready to rise at all hours to serve their masters, would persist for many centuries: only quite recently did a private sleeping room come to be regarded as a privilege rather than a deprivation.

A recreated medieval bedchamber (above) shows a curtained and canopied bed standing on a damp-proof platform. Its hangings are suspended on cords from the roof in the customary manner. This represents a later medieval Flemish bedchamber at Walraversijde, near Ostend, Belgium, but similar beds were also commonly used by the wealthier householders of medieval Wales.

The characteristic Welsh cloak worn by this thirteenth-century spearman (right) probably doubled as a bed-cover at night, like the *brychan*. The *brychan* described by Gerald and others was perhaps rather larger than this, and probably resembled a Highland 'great plaid'. Indeed, Gerald describes one as being 'covered with stripes of various multicoloured cloths', which sounds very like plaid. Certainly these cloaks/bedcovers were highly prized: a king's *brychan* was valued at 120 silver pennies, a nobleman's at half as much.

# Castles of discomfort?

Travellers along the busy A5, glimpsing the stark and dramatic ruins of Castell Dinas Brân on a windswept hilltop high above Llangollen — and even those hardier souls who actually climb to view its remains — may be pardoned for believing that this can never have been anything but a comfortless fortress, built for warfare only and certainly devoid of anything resembling interior decoration. Yet a closer inspection reveals traces of the finely carved stone vaulting which once roofed the gatehouse passage, and in many places sharp eyes can still distinguish remnants of the plasterwork which once covered the interior walls of the hall, keep, kitchen and chambers. For, like castles everywhere, Dinas Brân was a residence as well as a fortress. Its owners valued comfort and display as well as defence, and equipped their castle with an unusually generous number of lavatories. But like all ruined medieval castles — perhaps ninety per cent of all the castles in Wales — the present appearance of Dinas Brân provides little hint of the original colour, beauty and even comfort within its walls.

It is however in the stone castles built by English kings and barons, and Welsh princes, that the earliest evidence of interior decoration in Wales can still be seen. Much of this interior decoration has endured (if only as a faint reminder of its original splendour) because it was made of stone. Finely carved stone windows survive in castles such as Chepstow and Caerphilly, and some of these, at least in royal castles like Caernarfon, were glazed from the outset. At Caerphilly the early fourteenth-century hall is lined with sculpted wall columns resting on carved triple heads, said to represent King Edward II, his favourite Hugh Despenser, and some of their courtier friends.

The many surviving castle-building accounts of Edward I demonstrate clearly that a staff of expert craftsmen, including carvers, carpenters, plasterers and painters, set to work on the interiors of his castles even before their exteriors were fully completed. Special attention, naturally, was given to halls and royal bedchambers: but the interior walls of all living rooms of all castles would have been at least plastered, if not otherwise adorned. Medieval castle owners would no more have lived with bare stone walls than house owners today would tolerate walls of bare breeze-blocks.

Among the expert craftsmen employed by Edward were men like the carpenter Philip of Ewyas, from the Welsh borders, a specialist in hall roofs, and the Savoyard stone carver Albert of Menz, whose specialities included both windows and fireplaces. One of the finest examples of an early 'lateral' fireplace in Wales can be seen at Conwy Castle. Such fireplaces were set into the thickness of a wall, and linked to a chimney shaft rising through it, rather than placed centrally on the floor. By making it possible to heat a large number of chambers on several storeys, rather than only one or two large rooms on the ground floor, and by providing a new focus for display, they pointed the way forward both for interior comfort and interior design.

Castell Dinas Brân, Llangollen, Denbighshire (left), was built by the local Welsh rulers of Powys Fadog in the 1260s but finally abandoned within two decades. Even this comprehensively ruined castle still contains hints of its original interior splendour.

There are traces of original plasterwork in the chimney of Dinas Brân's D-shaped Welsh Tower (right), whose ground floor probably served as a kitchen for the adjacent castle hall. Remnants of original medieval wall plaster most often survive in sheltered crannies like this.

Carving, too, may survive in obscure nooks of castles, like this thirteenth-century foliage adorning a fireplace in the hall basement of Skenfrith Castle, Monmouthshire (above far left).

A finely carved thirteenth-century window in the great tower of Chepstow Castle, Monmouthshire (above centre), with part of a pair of sculpted arches which divided the great hall from the chamber beyond.

Edward II lent his master mason, Thomas de la Bataile, to his favourite, Hugh Despenser, to remodel the great hall at Caerphilly Castle (opposite). The early fourteenth-century windows were probably carved by him, and the central head of this trio (above) may represent Edward II himself.

A well-preserved lateral fireplace in an upper room in the King's Tower at Conwy Castle (left). The massive stone fire hood above the lintel helped to create an updraught for the chimney.

# A gallery of stone carvings

Carved stonework is probably the earliest surviving form of interior decoration in Wales. These eleventh- to fourteenth-century examples all come from what were originally interior rooms, but many have long been exposed to rain and wind. Battered by time and weather as most of them are, these carved decorations are not now as they originally appeared. In particular, many of them were undoubtedly brightly painted, adding to that now largely lost and forgotten element of the medieval interior — its bright colouring.

This stone head (right) was found at Castell y Bere, near Tywyn, Gwynedd, begun by Prince Llywelyn the Great of Gwynedd in the earlier thirteenth century. Simply but powerfully carved, it has bulging eyes recalling much older Celtic carved heads.

©NMW

Part of a carved door surround from Castell y Bere (above), apparently depicting a hand holding a spear or lance. Like other finely carved capitals recovered from the site, it testifies to the once splendid interior of this now remote and sadly ruined princely castle.

Probably the oldest surviving secular 'interior decoration' in Britain (above). This criss-cross pattern in white and orange plaster, dating from the late eleventh century, adorns an arched recess in the principal chamber of Chepstow Castle's great tower.

The head of a monarch found at Llywelyn the Great's now-vanished thirteenth-century castle of Deganwy (far left), near Conwy, perhaps depicts the prince himself.

This head of a bearded man (left) is one of a series of carved corbels lining the bishop's hall at St Davids Bishop's Palace, Pembrokeshire, built by Bishop Henry de Gower during the 1330s. The palace had one of the most elaborately embellished interiors in fourteenth-century Wales, and many traces of its decoration still survive.

A much weathered lion mask (above) can be seen in the basement vaulting of the Green Chambers at Denbigh Castle. Built around 1350, these chambers housed the finest apartments in the castle. This carving however comes from a basement probably used as a wine cellar or food store, demonstrating that carved decoration was not always confined to living rooms.

This beautifully carved and little worn fourteenth-century head of a woman (above) is thought to have come from Weobley Castle on the Gower peninsula. Perhaps it graced the solar, or private chamber, of this comparatively modest but well-decorated and comfortable home of the de la Bere family: Weobley was more a defensible courtyard house than a fortress.

## Adding the colour

By far the most important feature we have lost from medieval interiors is their vibrant colour, provided by wall paintings; wall hangings; bed hangings and other furnishing textiles; and painted timberwork, furniture and stone carvings. The bare stone walls, battered and age-blackened furnishings, and faded tapestries of surviving medieval and later interiors give an entirely misleading impression of their original appearance. It is an impression which has sunk so deep into public consciousness that attempts to evoke colourful historic interiors are often greeted with howls of outrage. Yet there is considerable surviving, pictorial, and documentary evidence for colourful interior decoration in medieval Wales.

## Medieval wall painting

The occupants of medieval homes did not like bare walls, or for that matter bare woodwork: so they limewashed or colourwashed them, and preferably — as the fourteenth-century poet Dafydd ap Gwilym urged — plastered and painted them as well.

In the poem below Dafydd might almost be describing the wall paintings at Chepstow Castle, which he may indeed have seen. Known from documentary evidence to have been painted in 1292, traces survive in the porch above the door of the great hall and in two chambers in Marten's Tower; both buildings were added to the castle by Roger Bigod, earl of Norfolk.

*'Is it worse that a white wall, the room's uneven surround, should be covered with lime (plaster) than if a pound were given to the painter — ingenious craftsman — to come and paint it with fair spots, to fill an empty space with golden colour and other beautiful hues, and the shape of fair shields?'*

Dafydd ap Gwilym

A fourteenth-century English painter holds his dishes of pigments, used to symbolize 'colour' in the earliest alphabetical encyclopaedia, the *Omne Bonum* of about 1350 (opposite).

Traces of two painted shields can be seen above the doorway to the great hall at Chepstow Castle (top). One of the shields is perhaps that of the Clare family. A reconstruction of this wall painting as it may originally have appeared (middle right). The wall colour is yellow ochre, a favourite pigment for medieval and later wall painters, and the shields 'hang' from painted *trompe l'œil* cords and hooks.

The wall paintings in two rooms in Marten's Tower have been reconstructed from surviving evidence (right). The lower walls are yellow ochre, with painted 'ashlaring' — imitation stonework — above, and a frieze of foliage at the top.

Bevis Sale for Cadw

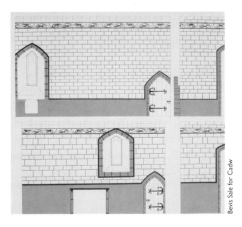

Bevis Sale for Cadw

©Peter Humphries

At Rhuddlan Castle, Denbighshire, Edward I's interior decorator was Stephen the Painter, who in 1282 was paid the comparatively large sum of 14s. for his labour and the purchase of pigments for the royal chamber. Stephen was an experienced professional from Savoy, who had earlier been employed to redecorate Westminster Hall for Edward's coronation. Stephen also probably decorated this room in the French castle of Chillon (above), whose contrasting pattern of red and white chevron work he perhaps repeated in Welsh castle interiors.

©English Heritage

### Figurative wall paintings

According to documents, the most elaborate painted decoration was generally commissioned for private chambers, which might be painted with figures of saints, hunting scenes and animals. This owl and magpie, painted in the vault of Bishop Gower's fourteenth-century screen in St Davids Cathedral (left), provide clues to the painted decoration of his palace nearby.

Though many figurative paintings survive in Welsh churches, none have so far been found in a medieval Welsh domestic interior. But allowing for its now much faded colours, this early fourteenth-century room at Longthorpe Tower, Cambridgeshire (above), gives a good idea of what a complete decorative scheme looked like. Decorated from floor to roof with biblical and moral scenes, birds and foliage, it was commissioned by a patron of only modest wealth. The painted chambers ordered by magnates like Edward I at Rhuddlan Castle and elsewhere were no doubt very much grander.

### 'Ashlaring'

'Ashlaring' — painting a plastered wall with lines (generally red) to imitate blocks of ashlar or fine masonry — is the commonest type of wall painting found in Wales. Sometimes the blocks are additionally adorned with flowers or foliage. Popular throughout thirteenth- and fourteenth-century western Europe, this fashionable style of decoration was used not only to disguise roughly coursed walls, but also to decorate walls which were themselves of fine ashlar masonry — the imitation concealing the genuine article.

Original ashlaring survives in domestic contexts in many castles in Wales. It can be seen easily in the window reveals of the thirteenth-century western hall at Lamphey Bishop's Palace, Pembrokeshire (above). Some blocks have the red five-petalled flowers characteristic of ashlaring, with yellow ochre stems sweeping across the whole pattern. Some imitation joints are made with single lines, some double, and the courses of masonry are of random width. The medieval-style ashlaring favoured for Victorian churches and Gothic house interiors is unconvincing because, characteristically, the Victorians made it too regular.

© Charles Kightly

Ashlar decoration in the thirteenth-century style has recently been recreated at Pembroke Castle (right), based on surviving examples elsewhere in Wales. The masoning and flowers are based on nearby Lamphey. The martlet birds are a device of the Valence family, contemporary owners of Pembroke Castle, and the Valence shield above the fireplace (not shown here) is based on the Chepstow survivals (p. 17). Wall hangings in the Valence family colours have also been recreated.

The Pembroke Castle ashlaring, in red ochre over lime plastering, was painted following medieval methods (above). The straight lines were made with pigment-soaked string snaplines. All the indications are that ashlaring was done very rapidly. Close examination of original work indicates that flowers sometimes had incised outlines, perhaps made with the aid of a lead stencil, of which at least one British medieval example survives. But in practice, the infilling of petals was most easily done freehand.

### Hangings and furnishing textiles

Surviving traces of medieval domestic wall paintings are comparatively rare: medieval furnishing textiles, vital not only for interior colour but also for draught proofing and general comfort, have vanished altogether. Not one single trace of a Welsh domestic wall hanging, bed hanging, curtain or cushion survives from before 1400, yet contemporary documents and illustrations prove that such textiles played a crucial part in the medieval interior. An entire department of Edward I's royal wardrobe was devoted to transporting the king's furnishing textiles during his campaigns in Wales, complete with its own carts, packhorse-men and outriders.

For like many high-status interior furnishings, medieval furnishing textiles were essentially portable. Hangings like the 98 yards (90m) of saffron-coloured cloth ordered by Henry III in 1230, or the painted canvas hangings commissioned for Queen Eleanor at Conwy in 1283, could be used to line a royal pavilion on campaign; re-hung to brighten a castle chamber during a temporary visit; and moved on again with their owner to the next castle or palace. It is perhaps partly because of their portable nature, as well as their vulnerability to moth, damp, theft and changes of fashion, that so few early textile furnishings survive in Britain. But their importance must never be underestimated.

Woven tapestries are shown in this manuscript illustration of a fifteenth-century English room (left). Earlier medieval documents more often record hangings of single colour or 'rayed' (striped) cloth or canvas in Welsh contexts.

This room also has a tiled floor laid out in a simple pattern and resembling floors still surviving in Welsh abbeys and churches. Documents prove that by 1400 — and increasingly afterwards — floor tiles were another element adding colour to the interiors of Welsh castles and great houses.

### Coloured furniture

Painted timber furniture is another entirely lost and almost forgotten contributor of colour to Welsh medieval interiors. In fact not a single piece of Welsh domestic furniture earlier than the fifteenth century survives. Yet medieval interior decorators and their patrons were as blind to the beauty of bare timber as they were to the attractions of unplastered stone walls, and it is quite certain that much furniture was originally painted both to preserve and to adorn it.

A model on display at St Davids Bishop's Palace (above centre) recreates the interior of this richly decorated mansion as it may have appeared in the time of Bishop Henry de Gower, in the mid-fourteenth century. The colourful wall paintings, painted timberwork, textile-hung bed and tiled floor are all closely based on surviving Welsh or English evidence or contemporary illustrations.

This recreated thirteenth-century chest (above), copied from surviving English examples and decorated in authentic pigments and style with the heraldry of the Valence family, was made for the ashlared room in Pembroke Castle (p. 19).

# Late Medieval, Tudor and
# Early Stuart Interiors 1400–1660

# Conspicuous consumption and comfort

The period which turned out to be the golden age of Welsh great house interiors — as opposed to great house interiors in Wales — began with two momentous upheavals, the Glyn Dŵr uprising of 1400 until about 1410, and the Wars of the Roses between 1455 and 1485. But then followed a long period of peace and prosperity throughout the Tudor and early Stuart eras, ending only in 1642 with the outbreak of the Civil War.

From a social and therefore a house-building and interiors viewpoint, the most important development during this period was the steady rise of a Welsh (or at least Welsh-based) gentry and aristocracy. Among these were such late medieval grandees as Sir William ap Thomas and the Herberts of Raglan; their supporters and relations the Vaughans of Tretower; and Sir Rhys ap Thomas of Carew and Weobley. These were all ambitious men who did well out of the wars. Then came those Welshmen who did well out of

the Tudor peace: families like the Wynns of Gwydir, the Mostyns of Gloddaeth, the Salesburys of Rug, and the Mansels of Oxwich. The Acts of Union put the Welsh gentry on the same footing as their English counterparts, and the suppression of the monasteries enabled them to acquire additional lands. Elizabethan and Jacobean Welsh courtiers, merchants and adventurers — Sir John Perrot of Carew, Richard Gough of Bachegraig, Robert Wynn of Plas Mawr and Sir John Trevor of Plas Teg — in turn proclaimed their wealth, influence and status by building or continuously improving or updating houses, and their interiors.

What lay behind all this building — and interior decorating — was not exclusively 'conspicuous consumption': though what might more prosaically be called 'showing off' did indeed play a dominant role. For the new developments in interiors during this period were also aimed at providing their occupants with a considerably greater degree of comfort and convenience than their ancestors had experienced.

We enjoy a far greater knowledge of the interiors of this period than of its predecessor. A considerable

number of complete interiors survive, including some with little altered features like plasterwork and panelling, as do at least some original textiles and many wall paintings. Documentation is also more abundant, including contemporary descriptions of interiors and in particular the appearance of household inventories. Dated and sometimes priced, these room-by-room lists of furnishings and other house contents were generally made after the owner's death. Such documents often tell us much about furnishings and other movable interior decorations. From them we learn, for example, that in 1509 Raglan Castle boasted a set of tapestries 'of the story of Nebuchadnezzar', 76 yards (69.5m) long. In 1536 the contents of Lamphey Palace included 'a short carpet of dornix lying upon the oyster table' and hangings of 'red and yellow say'; in 1592 the furnishings of Carew Castle ranged from 'four curtains of sad (dark) blue taffety fringed with silver, price thirty shillings' to 'an old cupboard cloth with a seam in the midst, price fourpence'; and in 1650 Richard ap John ap Evan of Denbighshire had wainscot panelling in his parlour, worth £2.

Raglan Castle, Monmouthshire (opposite), one of the grandest of all Welsh Renaissance houses, was begun by Sir William ap Thomas in the 1430s. It was developed into a magnificent fortress-palace by his son, Sir William Herbert, during the 1460s, and transformed into a great Elizabethan mansion with a long gallery by his descendant, the third earl of Worcester.

Less grand in scale than Raglan, Tretower Court, Powys (right), is essentially a late medieval fortified country house, supplanting the earlier castle which still stands nearby. Mainly built by Sir Roger and Sir Thomas Vaughan — relations of the Raglan Herberts — between about 1455 and about 1480, it was superficially updated by their descendants during the early seventeenth century.

Carew Castle, Pembrokeshire (above), also reflects development from a fourteenth-century fortress into a showy early Tudor mansion of about 1500. Lavishly updated by Sir Rhys ap Thomas, the Welsh power broker who assisted Henry VII to the throne, it was then fashionably modernized yet again by the flamboyant Elizabethan adventurer Sir John Perrot, who added a great three-storey long gallery range, overlooking the millpond.

Not all new Welsh Renaissance houses were in the country. Plas Mawr, in the centre of Conwy (above right), was built between 1576 and 1580 by Robert Wynn. This younger son of the rising Wynn family of Gwydir began his career as a soldier and diplomat in Europe, before taking his place among the north Wales gentry. The Flemish-style watchtower and crow-stepped gables of Plas Mawr recall his youthful travels in the Low Countries.

Plas Teg, near Hope, Flintshire (middle left) was built in about 1610 for Sir John Trevor, another younger son who prospered outside Wales. Copying the latest Jacobean London fashions, this exotic-looking mansion is one of a group of 'wonder houses' built by Welsh courtiers.

By no means all the houses built by the Welsh gentry in the fifteenth to the seventeenth centuries were on the scale of Raglan or Plas Teg. The great majority were smaller but modestly comfortable mansions-cum-farmhouses, built (especially along the borders) in the timber-framed tradition. Beautifully restored Upper House, Discoed, near Presteigne, Powys (middle right), has been tree-ring dated to 1536, the year of the first Act of Union. Penarth, near Newtown, Powys (bottom left), still a farmhouse, has a pair of wings of about 1600 added to a fifteenth-century hall. Plasau Duon, Clatter, Powys (bottom right), built just before the Civil War and the home of the parliamentarian Major-General Mytton, has the two-storey porch characteristic of seventeenth-century Montgomeryshire houses.

# Old rooms, new rooms

In higher status houses at least, during the fifteenth to seventeenth centuries there was a marked change in emphasis in the comparative importance and decoration of living rooms, and new types of room appeared. The hall gradually declined into an entrance foyer or a servants' eating room. Its place as the chief 'show room' was taken by the great chamber or dining parlour, or in the very grandest houses by the long gallery, that epitome of Elizabethan grandeur. The 'middling sort' followed the fashion as much as they could afford, or their houses would allow: the poor ignored it altogether.

The hall survived, however, at the bottom and the top end of the social scale. In the simplest one-roomed houses, it remained the sole living space. In the very grandest mansions, a great hall was used for lavish public ceremonies, though most other socializing took place in a hierarchy of other reception rooms.

*According to a description written soon after the Civil War, Raglan Castle boasted not only* 'a stately Hall, sixty-six feet long and twenty-eight broad, having a rare geometrical roof built of Irish oak', *but also a* 'Parlour, being 49 feet long and 21 feet broad ... noted as well for the inlaid wainscott and curious carved figures, as also for ... rare and artificial stone work ... in a fair and large compass window', *and a* 'Dining Room, of the same proportions as the Parlour'.

The hall at Plas Mawr, Conwy (above), finished in 1580, has a fine fireplace overmantel and plastered ceiling: but by then the hall had already declined in status, and a hundred years later this room had become a servants' dining room, furnished only with a few stools and chairs (including a 'high chaire for a child to sit in', worth 1s.) This situation is reflected in inventories from all over seventeenth-century Wales. The social dominance of the hall had been usurped by the great chamber or dining parlour.

The windows in the hall at Raglan Castle contained stained glass decorated with family coats of arms, as shown in this manuscript illustration (above). It depicts heraldry recorded at Raglan and Chepstow castles.

When Gwilym ap Gruffudd (whose service to Henry VII at Bosworth earned him the sheriffdom of Caernarvonshire for life) built Cochwillan, near Bethesda, Gwynedd, in about 1500 (above), the medieval great hall still reigned supreme as the principal show room of most houses. This view looks towards the high table end, where the owner and his honoured guests dined on a raised dais, with a canopy of honour (here timber-framed) above their heads. After dinner they could retire through one of the flanking doors to the principal chamber, customarily sited at this end of the hall.

The principal chamber at Gloddaeth, near Llandudno (left), is in the traditional position behind the high-table end of the hall. Its importance is emphasized by a fine painted fireplace. Preserving one of the most elaborately decorated sixteenth-century interiors in Wales, Gloddaeth was built by another family who prospered under the Tudors, the Mostyns. Sometimes referred to as parlours, such ground-floor chambers might double as best or guest bedrooms, a use which persisted for many centuries in lesser houses.

The well-lit first-floor great chamber at Plas Mawr (above) as it may have appeared in about 1580, was from the outset the grandest show room in the mansion. The large windows were a measure of wealth, and ensured that the decorated interiors could be clearly seen. Rooms called great chambers had long existed in addition to great halls, but had served as semi-private receiving rooms or 'master bedrooms'. In Elizabethan times, great chambers progressively superseded the hall as the room where the family ate ceremonially and strove to impress their guests.

In addition to all its other state rooms, Raglan Castle also possessed a long gallery (below), reconstructed here with the furnishings it is known or believed to have contained in the late Elizabethan period (though the floor would certainly have been covered throughout with matting). It was '126 feet long, having many fair windows, but most pleasant was the window at the furthermost end.' One of their purposes was to provide space for exercise in bad weather and pastimes such as needlework, which required good light. Nevertheless, such long galleries were essentially show rooms, where fine panelling and plasterwork, costly tapestries and hangings, and portraits of real or sometimes imaginary ancestors could be displayed — in fact, the original picture galleries.

The long gallery added to Powis Castle, near Welshpool, in 1592–99 (right) is probably the finest surviving in Wales. By that time no mansion interior of any pretension could be considered complete without this fashionable appurtenance. Other complete long galleries can be seen in Wales, for example at Chirk Castle, Wrexham, and St Fagans Castle, near Cardiff, and remains survive at Carew Castle — whose unfinished gallery would have been 147 feet (44.8m) long — Oxwich Castle, Gower, and elsewhere.

# Fireplaces

Wall-set fireplaces with chimneys — replacing smoky, dangerous and inconvenient central floor hearths — survive in castles in Wales from the twelfth century. By the middle of the fifteenth century, they were also being installed in gentry houses, and rapidly became the focus of more and more elaborate decoration.

The intricate embellishment of timber chimney pieces followed, continuing a decorative tradition long established in many parts of Wales — the use of expertly carved and often painted timberwork.

At first the replacement of an old-fashioned floor hearth by a new wall-set fireplace — as was probably done here at Penarth Fawr, near Pwllheli, Gwynedd (above left), during the sixteenth century — was perhaps in itself a sufficient status symbol, and some early fireplaces were left undecorated.

Soon, however, owners could not resist embellishing their fireplaces. That at Hafoty, Anglesey (left), dating perhaps from about 1535, is carved with the Latin motto of the Bulkeley family (reading in English, 'If God is for us, who is against us') and was originally painted in red and faux marbling.

The carved and painted stone fireplace in the hall at Gloddaeth, near Llandudno (bottom left and right), is of about the same date as that at Hafoty. It may have been carved by the same craftsman, but is even more elaborate. It bears both the Mostyns' Welsh motto *Heb dduw heb ddim duw a digon* (Without God, nothing: With God, plenty) and the Latin royal motto, *Honi soit qui mal y pense* (Shame on him who thinks evil of it). The unusual stone fender is also probably original. The decoration on the fireplace includes a grotesque figure drinking from a golden cup.

By the Elizabethan period, decoration had spread from the fireplace itself to its surroundings. These finely carved humanoid figures (right) — a female caryatid and male atlante — flanked the carved fireplace of Raglan Castle's long gallery, which was probably originally painted. Like so many 'antique work' decorations at this period, they were copied directly from an imported pattern book.

Surrounded by fluted columns and tier upon tier of decoration, this extraordinarily rich chimney piece is now at Badminton House, Gloucestershire

(below), but may have originally been installed in the great parlour at Raglan Castle, noted for its 'inlaid wainscott and curious carved figures'. Its style dates it to the mid-seventeenth century, just before the destruction of Raglan in the aftermath of the Civil War.

Overmantels were generally the most elaborately decorated elements of Elizabethan and Jacobean fireplaces. This fantastically carved overmantel, with its ruffed and bearded attendants, was removed during repairs to Far Hall at Llanddewi Ystradenni, Powys (below right).

Cruder but endearing painted plaster caryatids of about 1580, flanking the badge and initials of Elizabeth I, decorate the overmantel above the great chamber fireplace at Plas Mawr, Conwy (below).

# Carved and painted timberwork

The tradition of fine wood carving was well established in medieval Wales, particularly in the north-east and all along the borderlands, where timber for carving was more easily available than workable stone. Glorious pre-Reformation wood carving still survives in the roofs and rood screens of many churches in Denbighshire, Flintshire and Powys.

Wood carvers would have worked on the interiors of Welsh houses and castles as well as churches. But when doctrinal fashion turned against church embellishment after the 1540s, they doubtless took on domestic contracts all the more readily.

What is not always so easy to see today, however, is that carved timberwork was frequently also painted: like wall paintings, textiles and plasterwork, it made Welsh Renaissance interiors quite as colourful as those of the medieval age.

The rood screen of about 1500, in the remote little Black Mountains church of Partrishow, Powys (left), would originally have been brightly painted as well as carved.

A craft-proud carpenter carved these pictures of his tools on the porch of Old Impton, near Presteigne, Powys (above). The timber was tree-ring dated to 1543.

Roof timbers in fifteenth- and early sixteenth-century houses were frequently both decoratively shaped and carved, as at Penarth Fawr (middle left) and on the braces of the magnificent hammerbeam hall roof at Cochwillan (middle right).

Sometimes the roof carving was markedly more elaborate over the high-table end of the hall, to emphasize the status of those who sat there. The shaped late medieval timbers at Nantclwyd House, Ruthin (left), were revealed by the removal of a Renaissance plaster ceiling.

Timber partition walls and screens were also elaborately carved, such as that which divided the hall from the passage and service rooms at Cochwillan (above). Similarly, at Gloddaeth (right), the screen behind the high table — intended to enhance its dignity — was decorated with carved arcading and cresting.

Post and panel partition screens were often painted as well as carved in Welsh houses, and a few of these painted timber screens still survive, though not in their original locations. These sections of a painted screen from Rhiwlas, Bala, Gwynedd (below), dated 1574, are now in St Fagans National History Museum.

The magnificent late sixteenth-century carved, painted and galleried Welsh screen from Cefn Mably mansion, near Newport (right), now re-erected in the medieval hall of Berkeley Castle, Gloucestershire.

The Rhiwlas and Cefn Mably screens were at least saved: this picture tells a sadder story. The painted screen from Plas Dolben, Llangynhafal, Denbighshire (below), was photographed lying amid the rubble of the demolished house, and its present whereabouts are unknown.

Preserved within a later cupboard, this elaborately carved and painted column head topped one of the hall aisle posts at Egryn, near Llanaber, Gwynedd (below right), where much other carved woodwork and traces of colouring also survive. Its earliest phases are tree-ring dated to 1507–10. The National Trust has recently acquired Egryn.

# Wall paintings

Wall paintings were clearly a very popular form of interior decoration in late medieval, Tudor, and early Stuart Wales. Survivals were once thought to be rare: but recent and ongoing investigations have (sometimes literally) uncovered many more examples, often in quite modest dwellings as well as high-status mansions. More Welsh domestic wall paintings no doubt await discovery, recording, and wherever possible conservation. The unstable, damp-prone and now often fragile plaster on which they were painted makes them among the most vulnerable and threatened evidence of the Welsh Renaissance coloured interior.

Among the most important recent discoveries are these traces of teardrop- or leaf-shaped painting in the north range of Tretower Court. They decorated the infill of a timber roof truss (above) — itself originally painted red — above what were probably guest chambers added by Sir Roger Vaughan during the 1460s. Doubtless part of a more complex scheme whose other elements have now vanished, they are painted in red lead pigment over lime-plastered mud and straw render (right). If (as is likely) they coincide with the date of the original building, they are the earliest recorded examples of decorated mud and straw render in Britain.

© Paine & Stewart

The great Elizabethan wall paintings at Gloddaeth are among the largest, best-preserved and most magnificent domestic survivals anywhere in Britain. The grandest, above the dais for the high table in the hall (top left), has as its centrepiece (top right) the Royal Arms of Queen Elizabeth I, dated 1584, with the loyal inscription 'God Save our nobel Queene Elizabeth and sende hir longe to reigne'. It is flanked by family heraldry (above right) amid strapwork, columns, and 'antique' grotesques. Though less colourful, the painting at the opposite end of Gloddaeth's hall (above left) also features heraldry, amid print-like black-on-white foliage.

A sixteenth-century wall painting has been recreated at the Old Market Hall, Llanidloes, Powys (right), as part of a permanent display on timber buildings there. Following contemporary practice, it is painted freehand in four authentic pigments over limewashed timbers and panels. The motifs are copied from surviving local originals.

A charming one-colour wall painting of a girl in the costume of the 1560s, from Cold Knap Farm, Barry, Vale of Glamorgan (far left). She holds a wedding bouquet, and may originally have formed part of a marriage scene covering the whole wall.

The classical motifs in many Elizabethan and Jacobean high-status wall paintings, as in contemporary wood and stone carvings and textile hangings, were copied directly from prints or woodcuts in imported books. This 1602 mirror-image 'antique work' wall painting originally adorned Thomas Mathew's study at Castellymynach, Creigiau, near Cardiff (top right).

Yet by no means all Welsh wall paintings were so precise or academic. This now fragmentary sixteenth-century painting at Upper House, Discoed (left), is more typical of the freehand style and limited palette of paintings in lesser gentry mansions and farmhouses. The wattle and daub of the wall on which it was painted can be clearly seen.

Where interior walls were timber-framed, the painted design normally covered the timbers and the plastered infill panels alike, often without making any distinction between the materials. An intricate and accomplished decorative scheme (bottom left and right), apparently imitating an Italian silk wall hanging, was discovered in 1987 beneath later panelling at Althrey Hall, Bangor Is-coed, Wrexham. Its likely date is the 1550s and — uniquely in Britain — it incorporates portraits, probably of the owner, Elis ap Richard (d. 1558), and his wife, Jane Hanmer.

# Hangings and furnishing textiles

From the late medieval period until the mid-seventeenth century, textile interior decorations — wall hangings, bed hangings, carpets (which were almost invariably placed on tables rather than on floors), cushions and the rest — remained as popular as they had been before 1400. Though there are very few survivors, and these are nearly always from the very top of the range, better documentation now allows us a much clearer idea of the types of textiles favoured, and even their comparative cost. Swatches of these textiles can be found inside the cover flaps.

## Tapestries

Historic wall hangings are sometimes loosely called tapestries, but in fact tapestries are a very specific kind of textile, in which the horizontal threads, or 'weft', are of many colours, interwoven with the single 'warp', or vertical thread, only where the pattern requires. This process was extremely time consuming and laborious, especially when the pattern was very complex, and tapestries were never cheap. Until the mid-seventeenth century they were always imported, generally from Flanders. At the end of the sixteenth century, a single yard of 'rich tapestry with personages' (human figures), incorporating real gold thread, could cost as much as £2 16s., more than four months' wages for a farm labourer at the time. Even the very cheapest sort of 'coarse verdures' (with a repeating foliage pattern) cost 2s. a yard.

Sets or 'chamberings' of real tapestries were thus tremendous status symbols: and it is indeed for this reason that some examples have survived, while cheaper materials have largely vanished. Far too expensive to discard, tapestries were often displayed for centuries as evidence of a family's long-standing wealth and noble ancestry. During the fifteenth to seventeenth centuries they are recorded only in the very greatest Welsh mansions like Carew Castle and Raglan Castle: in 1507 Raglan boasted not only a set of white verdure 168 yards (154m) long, but also two 'story' tapestries each 76 yards (70m) long, and three more chamber sets of red and green verdures. Less opulent houses, like Lamphey Palace in 1536, might possess a few single tapestries in their best rooms, but tapestries of any kind were well beyond the reach of most Welsh householders, who turned for their hangings to cheaper materials.

A thirteen-piece set of tapestries of the Story of Gideon, in the long gallery of Hardwick Hall, Derbyshire (above), was bought second-hand in 1592 for over £320. Raglan had at least two 'story' sets, of Nebuchadnezzar and of an unknown character, Ide. Sets of tapestries for high-roofed rooms like those at Hardwick and Raglan had to be deep as well as long, still further increasing their fabulous cost.

## Woollen hangings

From the fifteenth until the mid-seventeenth century — when it was superseded by a local speciality, Welsh flannel — much the most popular woollen material recorded for textile furnishings was 'say'. This light but closely woven fabric retailed at about 1s. 6d. per yard in 1582. Recreated by modern Welsh weavers and dyers, this striped say 'banker', or seat cover, and red say 'dorser' brighten the high-table end of the hall — always a focus for interior decoration — at Barley Hall, York. Say came either in single colours — in 1536 the great chamber at run-down Lamphey had a 'green say hanging eaten with moths' — or in contrasting 'paled' vertical stripes. Lamphey also had hangings of striped red and green and red and yellow say.

© Barley Hall

## 'Dornix'

© Charles Kightly

© NMW

Taking its name from its place of origin, Doornik (Tournai) in Flanders, 'dornix' was cheaper than say, selling in 1582 at 6d. to 1s. per yard. As this original sample shows (top left), it had a linen ground warp, with repeating two- or three-colour wool patterning, generally of flower motifs.

Recreated dornix hangings, copied from the original above, were used to furnish the great chamber at Plas Mawr (above left). They have the all-round fringing characteristic of Elizabethan hangings. This cheap but attractive 'poor man's tapestry' was popular from the later fifteenth until the mid-seventeenth century.

Dornix was also widely used — as at Lamphey, Carew and elsewhere — for bed hangings, coverlets, cushions and table carpets. These recreated seventeenth-century bed hangings at Kennixton farmhouse, St Fagans National History Museum (above right), are copied from an original dornix dated 1653.

## Painted cloths

At the cheapest end of the hangings market were 'stained' or 'painted cloths', size-treated linen canvas painted with scenes to imitate tapestry, or stencilled with repeated motifs imitating damask hangings (as in this Elizabethan original, left). Selling new at around 6*d.* per yard, whole cloths could be bought second-hand for a few pennies.

Though extremely popular with thrifty householders from medieval times until the Georgian period, painted cloths deteriorated rapidly, and are now so rare as to be almost forgotten. This is the only known Welsh survivor, from Caerau, Llanfair-yng-Nghornwy, Anglesey (below left). It probably dates from the eighteenth century.

An even rarer survival, perhaps unique in Britain, this section of plaited rush wall hanging was discovered above a seventeenth-century plastered ceiling at Upper Dolley, Ackhill, near Presteigne, Powys (below). Found still nailed to oak battens on the wall top, part of the hanging had been left in position when the ceiling was installed below, possibly in the 1640s — so the hanging must be earlier.

# New fashions: panelling

Wood is draught proof, a poor conductor of heat, and does not suffer much condensation: so interior walls were from an early date sealed with timber for comfort.

But decorative panelling or 'wainscotting' — from a word meaning 'good quality oak planking' — became fashionable only in the earlier sixteenth century, and generally popular in wealthier Welsh houses by the 1590s, continuing in changing styles well into the Georgian period. Although

fixed panelling might suggest a more settled way of life than portable wall decorations, contemporary inventories sometimes valued it as a movable. It could be, and was, sold — or, during the Civil War, plundered — for reuse in other houses, often involving drastic and still obvious alteration.

Earlier panelling sometimes perpetuated the older Welsh wood-carving tradition: the delightful mythical beasts on this carved field panelling recall the style of pre-Reformation Denbighshire rood screens. Dating from about 1570 or earlier, and now in Llanynys church near Ruthin, Denbighshire (above), it was originally made for nearby Bachymbyd Fawr, home of Colonel William Salesbury.

A more metropolitan fashion for panel carving was the linenfold motif, originally derived from Flanders. It is used in panelling of about 1560 in the principal bedroom at Llanvihangel Court, near Abergavenny, Monmouthshire (left).

Both carved and plain early panelling was often originally painted. In the long gallery at Powis Castle (right), the early seventeenth-century wainscotting is cleverly painted to imitate fielded, or facetted, panelling.

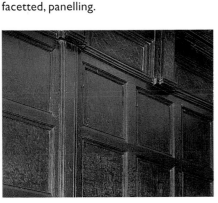

Superior grades of panelling might alternatively be inlaid with contrasting coloured woods. In the morning room — originally the parlour — of Llanvihangel Court (above), a frieze of oak panelling inlaid with lighter holly and darker ebony in diamond shapes divides the plastered ceiling from the plain panelling below.

Surmounted by a gallery and a geometrical plaster ceiling, this wainscotting at Old Gwernyfed, near Hay-on-Wye, Powys (below left), follows the early seventeenth-century fashion for architectural panelled rooms, which imitated the columned exteriors of Classical buildings.

The magnificent 1640s panelling of the dining room at Gwydir Castle, near Llanrwst, Conwy (below right), has

travelled further than most. Bought by the millionaire, William Randolph Hearst, and transported to the U.S.A., the entire room was rescued by the present owners and restored to its original setting. Its lavishly decorated wainscotting points the way to the even more sumptuous panelled rooms of the later seventeenth century. Above the panelling is an embossed leather frieze.

© NTPL/Andreas von Einsiedel

© RCAHMW

# New fashions: plasterwork

Though walls had been plastered since the Middle Ages, cast and moulded decorative plasterwork was originally an Italian fashion, first introduced to Britain by Henry VIII and Cardinal Wolsey for their sixteenth-century palaces. Partly due to the difficulty and expense of engaging practitioners of the new craft, it did not appear in Welsh mansions until the 1560s. But when it did, it produced some truly amazing results.

Plas Mawr, Conwy, has much the most spectacular array of early decorative plasterwork in Wales, and indeed one of the finest in all Britain. Seven of its rooms retain surviving plasterwork, and five of them have a complete set of ceiling, wall frieze and fireplace overmantel. The 'Chamber over the Brewhouse' (opposite) was probably the bedchamber of Robert Wynn, the builder of the house. It contains one of the most elaborate schemes, including an overmantel dated 1577 decorated with Wynn's heraldic arms and initials, and a wall frieze and geometric ceiling sprinkled with embossed grotesques and heraldic emblems.

Such emblems appear throughout the house. Wynn's own family device, the spread eagle (top), and the family badge of his wife Dorothy Griffith, the 'severed Englishman's head' (above), are most prominent. Other emblems include the Tudor rose, the bear and ragged staff of Queen Elizabeth's favourite, Lord Leicester, and the badges of the princes of Gwynedd. A parade of charming caryatids in acanthus-leaf skirts (left) appears in the main public rooms. Here too the original colouring of the plasterwork has been restored, a reminder that plastering also played its part in the colourful interior.

The flat geometrical ceilings in four rooms at Llanvihangel Court, dating from around 1600 but perhaps partially restored in the early twentieth century, also bear a marked resemblance to those of Plas Mawr. The hall ceiling (above left) is decorated with Tudor roses and fleurs-de-lys. The angular ribwork in the morning room (above right) resembles the great chamber ceiling at Plas Mawr.

The itinerant plasterers Wynn employed at Plas Mawr went on to work in other Welsh mansions, as the repetition of similar styles and the reuse of their particular emblem moulds there demonstrates. Among these mansions was Maenan Hall, near Llanrwst (above), where the wonderfully elaborate hall plasterwork is dated 1582, two years after the completion of Plas Mawr. Plas Mawr has flat ceilings purpose-built for plasterwork: but Maenan was an older house, and there the plasterwork covers but does not conceal the main members of the great timber roof.

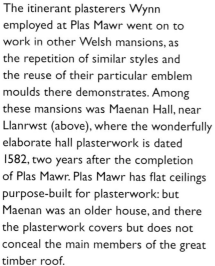

This utterly astonishing seventeenth-century barrel-vaulted plaster ceiling (above) survives only by chance. It depicts the labours of Hercules amid the signs of the Zodiac. Originally installed at Emral Hall, Worthenbury, Wrexham, both the ceiling and adjacent panelling were auctioned in 1930 and bought by the architect, Sir Clough Williams-Ellis, for just £13. Six years later Emral was demolished, but the room and its ceiling remain as the glories of the Hercules Hall at Portmeirion, Sir Clough's famous architectural fantasy village near Porthmadog, Gwynedd.

# Personalized decoration

The late medieval love of heraldry, symbolism and personal devices grew even stronger during the sixteenth and seventeenth centuries. In Wales especially, the gentry and lesser folk alike were known for their preoccupation (or indeed obsession) with noble ancestry, pedigrees and family relationships. Certainly the personalization of interior decoration with heraldry, family mottoes, and the devices of real or imaginary ancestors survives particularly frequently in Welsh interiors.

© NMW

© National Library of Wales

© By kind permission of Nancy, Lady Bagot

This portrait of Thomas ap Ieuan ap David of Arddynwent, Flintshire, painted about 1610 (above), exemplifies the Welsh love of symbolism. It displays not only the many quarterings of his family arms, but also a branch of olive, and a robin representing Christ, chanting a Latin extract from the Psalms: 'Abandon evil and do good.' Such religious devices joined the symbolic vocabulary of pious Welshmen after the Reformation.

The gatehouse fireplace overmantel at Gwydir Castle (above right), is emblazoned with the arms of the Wynn family.

The early sixteenth-century arms of the Mostyn family are carved and painted on the chamber fireplace at Gloddaeth (above left). Heraldry and mottoes were also frequently applied to timberwork,

textiles, plasterwork, and indeed every possible form of interior decoration.

This biographical portrait of William Salesbury of Rug and Bachymbyd Fawr, painted in 1632 (bottom left), includes his arms, his age, his personal Welsh motto, 'What God wills shall come to pass', and a picture of the privateer, *Barque Wylloby*, on which he served in the West Indies. 'Old Blue Stockings', as he was known, later achieved fame as the obstinate defender of Denbigh Castle during the Civil War.

At Penarth Fawr, near Pwllheli, a humbler form of personalization cut on a timber beam survives: the initials of John and Jane Wynn (using the seventeenth century 'I' for 'J') and the date February 20th 1656 (below). It may commemorate a marriage or, more likely, an alteration to the house.

© Charles Kightly

# Later Stuart and Georgian
# Interiors 1660–1840

# Elegance and divergence

The two centuries of domestic peace that followed the Civil War saw the appearance in Wales of the country house and the town house as we now understand them. Until then, a gentry house had usually been either the working centrepiece of an agricultural estate, or a converted fortress. But the new houses were purpose-built mansions designed to accommodate their owners amid comfortable, elegant, and above all impressive surroundings, often enhanced by ornamental parkland. Such houses did not develop organically from earlier buildings, but were architect designed from the outset in the new symmetrical style. They had impressive centrally placed entrances, and grand staircases rising to a variety of elegant reception rooms and tiers of heated bedrooms. As the period progressed, working areas and servants' quarters were increasingly tidied away out of sight.

Many earlier gentry houses had been grander and more richly decorated versions of the dwellings of neighbouring farmers. But these new mansions, in both their design and their interior decoration, followed the successive tides of fashion which swept across Britain, often from sources elsewhere in western Europe. There was very little to distinguish the interior of such a mansion in Wales from its counterpart in Somerset or Derbyshire.

Further down the social scale, those with neither the wealth nor perhaps the wish to follow the new fashions might move into outdated older gentry houses, and many late medieval or Renaissance Welsh mansions have survived because they became farmhouses. Others continued to build and decorate houses in traditional styles, in some cases styles which had persisted since the early Middle Ages. As the differences between the houses of rich and poor increased, so does the information available to us about the houses of ordinary people. Eyewitness descriptions (from the contemptuous or pitying to the admiring) and paintings of 'romantic peasant interiors' augment the growing number of inventories and other documents.

More important still, the oldest surviving dwellings of upland smallholders and agricultural or industrial labourers date from this period. Some of these still display the one-room interiors and central floor hearths which — a few details apart — would have been familiar to Gerald of Wales.

Yet despite this growing divergence between the house interiors of rich, middling and poor, fashions in interior decoration continued to filter down from the top, as perhaps they have done since interior decoration began. For example, those who could not afford the fashionable new wallpapers, bought in towns and at first very costly, simply adapted an older tradition by painting imitations of them on their walls.

Great Castle House, Monmouth (left), was built in 1673 in the new symmetrical style. It is one of several new mansions raised by the marquesses of Worcester to replace Raglan Castle, rendered uninhabitable as a result of the Civil War.

Tredegar House, near Newport (right), one of the very finest Restoration mansions in Britain, was largely rebuilt during the 1660s by the immensely wealthy Morgan family.

Nanteos, near Aberystwyth (top left), was begun in 1739 for the Powell family. Designed in the Italianate style, it exemplifies the Georgian fashion for imposing entrance porticoes and flat-fronted, box-like exteriors, with the roof gables concealed by parapets.

Previously grand but now unfashionable houses were often let. Plas Mawr, Caernarfon (top right), was divided up,

and squatters are shown living there in this sketch of 1808 by John Nixon.

By no means all medieval Welsh castles fell into disuse. The interiors of Powis, Chirk, Fonmon and several others continued to be updated in the latest styles during the later seventeenth and eighteenth centuries. Picton Castle, near Haverfordwest (above left), dates originally from about 1300. It was

remodelled in the Georgian style during the 1750s, and in the 1790s a new Regency block was added.

The simple interior of Nant Wallter (above right), a thatched and mud-walled cottage, illustrates the furnishings of a country labourer's dwelling. Built in about 1770 at Taliaris, Carmarthenshire, it has now been re-erected at St Fagans National History Museum.

# A proliferation of rooms

### Entrance halls and staircases

The old-style great hall was already long redundant when this period began. In the new mansions a 'hall' was an entrance hall, the meaning it has retained to this day. Opening directly from the central main entrance, such halls were intended to stun the arriving visitor with the owner's elegant taste. Though generally sparsely furnished, they were often decked out with paintings and sculptures acquired during a Grand Tour of Europe.

From the hall usually rose a grand stair, sometimes dividing into two as it ascended majestically to the best bedrooms or elegant reception rooms off a first-floor landing. To enhance the effect, stairway walls were often lined with large family portraits or 'ancestral' tapestries.

Staircases themselves were elaborately carved and decorated, especially in the earlier part of the period. This fine staircase with its barley-sugar-twist balusters was installed in the central entrance hall of Llanvihangel Court (above right), when it was remodelled as a symmetrical mansion during the 1670s. Most unusually, it is made entirely of rich red yew wood.

The 'Staircase Hall' at Fonmon Castle, Vale of Glamorgan (right), was created during the 1760s, when this originally thirteenth-century fortress was comprehensively updated for a fashionable young owner. As so often happened, this remodelling coincided with a marriage to an heiress.

## Dining rooms and drawing rooms

The living room functions of the great hall and its successor, the great chamber, were meanwhile taken over by a variety of new reception rooms, which offered an opportunity to display new decorative fashions. In houses of any pretension, the dining room was used for no other purpose. From here, diners retired to the drawing room, sometimes still called the 'withdrawing room'. This might be the intimate sitting room it later usually became, or alternatively one of the most richly decorated rooms in the mansion.

© NTPL/Andreas von Einsiedel

The White Drawing Room at Picton Castle, Pembrokeshire (above left) was created in about 1750, during the Georgian remodelling of the house: it remains unchanged apart from the colour of the painted panelling. When a new block in the Regency style was added forty years later, the Regency dining room took up one half of the ground floor and a new drawing room the other half. The two rooms have now exchanged roles (middle left).

When the interior of Chirk Castle, (middle right), home of the rich and powerful Myddeltons, was sumptuously revamped in the 1770s, it was given not only a new state dining room and a drawing room, but also the lavishly decorated Saloon. A remodelling of a pre-existing seventeenth-century great chamber, it had the highest status of all Chirk's Georgian reception rooms.

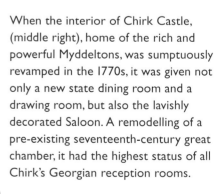

© NTPL/Andreas von Einsiedel

The dining room at Erddig, near Wrexham, added to the house in 1826–27 (left). A rather heavy interpretation of the then fashionable Greek Revival style, it has columned 'Doric' screens.

## Libraries and music rooms

Georgian ladies and gentlemen were expected to be people of taste as well as people of fashion. Among the specialized rooms which appear in mansions of this period was therefore the library or study, traditionally a male refuge from family life. Less frequently, a music room was included. It was often the preserve of the ladies, but was also used for select concerts and other formal entertaining.

The delightful round library or study at Picton Castle (above) still contains the ingenious joinery fitted by the London carpenter James Rich in about 1750: the columns between the book cupboards are doors which conceal secret shelving. The paint colour is modern.

The Rococo-style library (left), also called the Long Drawing Room, fulfilled both these functions at Fonmon Castle, and was the chief showpiece of the house. The medieval and seventeenth-century interiors were transformed during the 1760s for a squire brought up in fashionable London and Bath. Like the Philipps family at Picton, Robert Jones III of Fonmon employed specialist English interior designers for the work, in this case Thomas Paty of Bristol and his plasterer, Thomas Stocking.

This Georgian panelled room of the 1770s (left) later became the music room at Erddig, Wrexham. It now displays the collection of instruments and music-making devices assembled by Erddig's owners, the eccentric Yorke family.

# Changing fashions: Restoration and Georgian ceilings

Plastered ceilings reached new heights of Baroque lushness during the later seventeenth century. Flat geometric ceilings now gave way to ceilings with a 'coffered' effect, following the underlying roof structure. Swags of fruit and flowers, sometimes of extraordinary opulence, were now preferred to heraldic emblems and grotesques.

The extravagant ceilings of the Restoration period were a comparatively short-lived fashion in Britain. The Georgians — at least at first — preferred rather less crowded and more restrained Classical plasterwork, now once again applied to flat ceilings.

Great Castle House at Monmouth (top left), built in 1673 to replace Raglan Castle, has some of the finest Restoration ceilings in Britain. Three of them can be seen in this noble first-floor room, created in about 1700 by throwing together several separate chambers, each with its own distinctive coffered ceiling.

The most opulent of the ceilings is an amazing tour de force of the plasterer's art. The coffering is encrusted with leaves and flowers, and from the centre hang deep swags of foliage, built up in plaster over supporting armatures made of boiled leather (middle left).

Rather more restrained, though equally intricate, wreaths of fruit adorn the ceiling of the central first-floor room (above).

A cherub graces the richly encrusted ceiling of a ground-floor chamber at Great Castle House (bottom left).

By 1750, when the White Drawing Room was created at Picton Castle (above), a more restrained style was in fashion. A bust of Shakespeare, surrounded by a wreath of bay leaves picked out with gilding, was applied to a flat ceiling.

Fifteen or so years later, however, a head in a similar Classical style was given Rococo embellishments in the library ceiling at Fonmon Castle (above right). The twisted acanthus leaf was the hallmark of the Rococo style, which was described as 'Frenchified and effeminate' and widely condemned as an affront to robust British taste.

Towards the end of the eighteenth century, some plasterwork ceilings reverted to a heavy Roman Classical style, though the plaster might be painted and gilded all over, as here on the repainted Saloon ceiling at Chirk Castle (right).

# Changing fashions: panelling, fireplaces and paint

Like plaster ceilings, wall panelling in fashionable houses was extremely elaborate during the later seventeenth century. Thereafter it settled into a simpler, Classical style. Georgian panelling was nearly always made of pine or other softwoods instead of oak, and almost invariably painted. Fireplaces and overmantels, after a last burst of Renaissance exuberance, became smaller in scale. They remained decorative showpieces, but depended for their effect upon expensive materials like marble, with modestly sized but tastefully carved embellishments.

The fabulous Gilt Room of about 1670 at Tredegar House, Newport (above), is entirely encased in architectural panelling, grained to imitate walnut and gilded on all its raised framing and carving. Its focus is a spectacular fireplace of black-veined marble, carved with cherubs and swags of fruit and surmounted by a ceiling-height overmantel with barley-sugar-twist columns.

Of approximately the same date as the Tredegar piece but recalling earlier fashions, this painted and carved stone fireplace is at Great Castle House, Monmouth (right). Above the Stuart coat of arms at its centre is a painted plaster overmantel, bedecked with swags of fruit.

Monmouth, which had twice changed hands during the Civil War, was keen to demonstrate its loyalty after the Restoration. A delightful plaster overmantel, depicting Charles II (opposite), survives at the King's Head Inn, which also has a contemporary painted plaster ceiling.

Some later seventeenth-century and early Georgian panelling had very large fields, but this small-panelled wainscoting of about 1670 at Great Castle House (below left) depends for its effect on zig-zag framing. Prefiguring Georgian panelling, it is painted —though these are not the original colours.

The pine panelling of about 1750 in the White Drawing Room at Picton Castle, Pembrokeshire (bottom left), was probably originally painted either sage green or pea green (both modish Georgian colours) and picked out with gilding. The contemporary inlaid marble fireplace, like several others in the castle, is by the fashionable sculptor

Sir Henry Cheere. Its overmantel incorporates a painting of game, and is topped by a carved flower basket. The centrepiece of the fireplace depicts cherubs lighting a fire (below right). A larger Cheere fireplace, now in the dining room, has another wintery theme, with skating cherubs flanked by a bear and a beaver (bottom right).

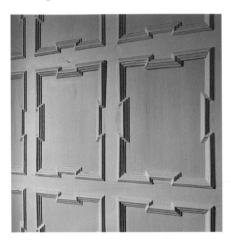

The library fireplace of about 1765 at Fonmon Castle is the outstanding example in Wales of that 'effete and insidious French import', the Rococo style. In a reaction against the strict rules and measured dignity of the earlier Classical style, convoluted free-style foliage surrounds the mirrored overmantel, while curled 'raffle' or acanthus leaves — an essential element of Rococo — protect the modesty of the gilded cherubs flanking the veined marble fireplace.

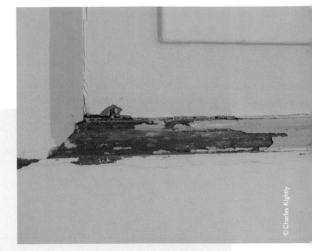

A paint scrape (above) showing the colours used on panelling of about 1750. Beneath the later grey finish is a patch of sage green, perhaps the original top coat. The traces of yellow-grey are possibly undercoat, and beneath that can be seen red primer, typical of the time and probably made from red ochre in oil.

Paint scrapes of historic finishes can however be very misleading, as the colours may not appear as they did originally. The effects of light may have altered the hue after the original application, and re-exposure may have changed it again. Newly exposed greens, for example, may develop a bluish tinge within weeks. The colours sold today as fashionable in the Georgian period are often derived from paint scrapes, and many are certainly far too muted. The only sure way to establish the original colour is by spectroscopic analysis of paint flakes.

*Swatches of favourite paint colours in the Georgian period can be found on the inside front cover flap.*

## Seventeenth- to nineteenth-century paints

Paints, limewashes and other colourants had of course always been used in Welsh interiors; but water-based distempers for ceilings and walls, and oil paints for panelling and other woodwork, came to be much more widely used during the Georgian era and afterwards. They were, however, very different from modern paints.

Today's industrially produced paints cost much the same whatever their colour, and standard paints by the same maker can usually be relied on to colour-match from tin to tin. The situation was very different during the seventeenth to nineteenth centuries, when paints were individually made up by the house painter from a huge variety of herbal or mineral pigments, mixed in a variety of combinations and media.

These ingredients varied very widely in cost. For example, in 1806 yellow ochre, possibly sourced from north-west Wales, cost less than 9d. per pound; blue verditer cost between 9d. and 3s. 3d. per pound; and green verdigris cost up to 7s. per pound. Indigo was vastly more expensive at up to 13s. a pound. The cost of ready-mixed tints bought from 'colourmen' likewise also varied widely from hue to hue.

In 1734, prices ranged from 4d. per pound for stone colour or oak colour; through around 1s. for olive colour or pea colour; up to 2s. 6d. for fine deep green.

So paints varied in price, not so much from colour to colour, but between particular hues of a colour. Needless to say, the hues made from the most expensive ingredients were also the most fashionable: not simply because they were costly, but also because they were less likely to fade, and produced the truest version of the colour required. But exactly what was meant by, for example, pea green would vary according to the mixing skills of the individual colourman, the favourite formula of the individual painter, and no doubt the taste of the client or his architect. Some bright and fashionable hues such as 'King's yellow', of which the ingredients included arsenic and sulphur, had distinct disadvantages. The author of *Every Man His Own House-Painter and Colourman* (1829) thought it 'necessary to caution the use of it, unless any one has a wish to be driven out of house and home…in that case, he has only to order one small apartment to be painted with King's yellow…for the smell cannot be confined, but sends its vile effluvia into every corner of the house…'

# Wall hangings and wallpapers

The popularity of painted panelling in fashionable interiors did not preclude the continued use of textile wall hangings. They were still the height of fashion for public rooms in the later seventeenth century. But by the end of the eighteenth century, such hangings had more often been relegated to bedchambers, where their draught-excluding properties were doubtless appreciated. Even there, however, they were by now being superseded in many upper- and middle-class houses by the newly fashionable wallpapers.

## Wall hangings

Tapestries were still expensive status symbols. They were still in use at Gwydir in the seventeenth century, and were still being displayed in the grandest living rooms at Abermarlais, Carmarthenshire, in 1756 and Llangedwyn, Powys, in 1772. Hangings of imported silk, cut velvet, or embossed and gilded leather, also expensive materials, were used in great houses in the late seventeenth century. More modest mansions like Faenol, Gwynedd, made do with hangings of 'homecloth' — Welsh flannel — according to a record of 1669. 'Plod' or tartan plaid, either Scottish or possibly made in Wales, was another relatively cheap material, sometimes recorded for bed hangings. Old Watstay, Denbighshire, home of the Wynn family and later rebuilt as Wynnstay, unusually had wall hangings of 'turkey work' in both its drawing room and several of its bedchambers in 1683.

According to inventories, however, by far the most popular textile for hangings both in Wales and England from the mid-seventeenth to the mid-eighteenth century was Kidderminster Stuff. This comparatively inexpensive fabric is recorded for example at Abermarlais in 1644; Plas Mawr, Conwy in 1665; Faenol in 1669; Old Watstay in 1683; and in minor rooms at Picton Castle in 1729. It was the speciality of Kidderminster, Worcestershire, later famous for its carpets. Kidderminster Stuff was still in use for bed-hangings at Llangedwyn in 1772. But by then the hangings had suffered the fate of many outdated and unfashionable furnishings — they had been exiled to a bedroom occupied by a gardener in an outbuilding. Many of the bedrooms in the main house, including those of the Wynn family and the upper servants, had paper hangings — or, as we should call them, wallpapers.

'Turkey work' or 'Norwich work' was an English-made fabric with a woollen pile on linen threads, woven to imitate the much pricier imported Turkish carpets. It is recorded in seventeenth-century Welsh interiors for cushions, table carpets and furniture upholstery, like this chair back of about 1680 (left), which was formerly at Hampton Court, Herefordshire. It was used for whole sets of wall hangings at Old Watstay, Denbighshire.

© Charles Kightly

Other Welsh mansions kept up the old tradition of using hangings that were lovingly, and lengthily, embroidered by the ladies of the house. These two panels are from a complete room set of five hangings from Bryncunallt, near Chirk, Wrexham, probably embroidered by Prudence Trevor in about 1710–20.

Thronged with exotic birds and flowers, perhaps in imitation of imported Indian chintzes, one panel features a gentleman on horseback, St Michael slaying the dragon, and a blue-gowned lady, possibly Queen Anne (below left). Another includes two fantastically dressed ladies, and a shepherd with his flock (below right).

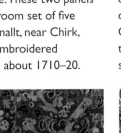

Kidderminster Stuff was a 'linsey-woolsey' mixture of linen and wool. A typical original sample has vertical warp stripes in alternate bleached and darker unbleached linen, with a two-colour woollen weft forming an all-over zig-zag pattern (above). Later Kidderminster Stuffs — exported as far afield as Sweden and the American colonies — were all-wool fabrics, but were made in similar designs.

Wall hangings and bed curtains of Kidderminster Stuff were recreated from the original sample for the 'Chamber over the Parlour' at Plas Mawr, Conwy (left). Recorded at Plas Mawr in the 1665 inventory, this distinctive textile was also widely used for cushion covers and table carpets.

## Wallpapers

Initially printed in inks using wood blocks, wallpapers or 'paper tapestries' had been produced since the late sixteenth century. Early papers were printed on small individual sheets, which might be pasted to canvas before being hung. Though specialist wallpaper shops existed in London by the end of the seventeenth century, their products were looked down on as mere cheap imitations of textile hangings, fit only 'to make the houses of more ordinary people look neat'. Only in the 1740s did wallpapers become really fashionable, partly because they could by then be block printed in vivid colours and in longer pieces, with 'repeats'. Particularly modish, following their installation in the London offices of the Privy Council, were 'damasks' or 'flocks', whose raised pattern was produced by scattering powdered wool onto varnish brushed through stencils.

Though considerably cheaper than silk or velvet hangings, flocks were comparatively expensive, retailing at between 4s. and 13s. per yard in the 1750s. So too were the imported and hand-painted 'India' or Chinese papers used on the walls and 'chimney board' of 'my Lady's Dressing Room' at Llangedwyn. This is the only type of wallpaper specifically described in the house inventory, perhaps because a single sheet of it (even at a 'special price' from Mr Chippendale) could cost 14s. Ordinary block-printed eighteenth-century papers were, of course, far cheaper, selling for as little as 4d. a yard.

Georgian flocked wallpaper survives at Clandon Park, Surrey (above).

Hand-painted Chinese wallpaper of about 1800 can be seen at Temple Newsam House, near Leeds (right).

**Fictive wallpapers: eighteenth- and nineteenth-century wall paintings**

Just as early wallpapers had often copied more expensive hangings, imitations of wallpapers — still comparatively costly in the late eighteenth and early nineteenth centuries — have been found painted directly onto walls in several houses in Wales. Some went even further in their use of paint, creating fictive portraits and yet more elaborate schemes.

An imitation of an imitation? This charming but inexpert wall painting, from a house in Presteigne, Powys (above), seems to imitate a late eighteenth-century 'Chinese style' wallpaper, of the type block printed in Britain to imitate the more costly hand-painted genuine article. It is now in the Judge's Lodging, Presteigne.

©RCAHMW

More expertly done and remarkably complete, this stencilled and painted imitation of an early nineteenth-century flowered wallpaper covers the walls of an attic room at Pibwrlwyd, Llangunnor, Carmarthenshire (left and above). The imitation border, at the base and sides of the paper as well as the top, faithfully follows contemporary papering practice. It is possible that the awkward shape of the walls here made it easier to paint than to paper them.

A strip of fictive wallpaper, possibly early Victorian and again with a border, was found at a house in Castle Street, Brecon, Powys (opposite).

In a tradition descended from the medieval shield paintings at Chepstow Castle (p. 17), this fictive hunting horn, musket and game bag of about 1780 hang at Upper House, Painscastle, Powys (right).

Wallpapers were not the only fashionable decorations to be imitated in paint. The ceiling at Court House, Glan Rhyd, Carmarthenshire (below), dated 1779, was painted to suggest the coloured Adam plasterwork ceilings then in vogue.

The most astonishing example of this craft in Wales, if not in all Britain, was discovered beneath later wallpaper at Elwy Bank, St Asaph, Denbighshire (a vulnerable building at the time of writing). Dating from about 1822–24, and attributed to the popular Welsh artisan painter, Hugh Hughes, it imitates in paint an entire fashionable room (far left) with fictive columns, curtains, portraits and patriotic figures: Edward, duke of Kent, father of Queen Victoria (left); Britannia (below left); and Admiral Nelson (below).

# Cottage and farmhouse interiors

Travellers' descriptions of Welsh cottages and farmhouses delighted and horrified armchair tourists throughout the eighteenth and early nineteenth centuries. By the 1770s, such descriptions were augmented by drawings and paintings of 'typical' Welsh cottage interiors, and their tone had changed. Georgian 'travellers of taste, in search of grand and stupendous scenery' were more inclined to view the inhabitants of rural Wales as 'noble savages', unspoilt by fashion, and their dwellings as uplifting examples of virtuous rural frugality.

> The whole was one dark room, with three windows so small,
> That the light down the chimney quite outstript them all.
> But this great relief came to soften their cares,
> Neither sober or drunk could they tumble down stairs.
> Two beds grac'd the mansion, which made it appear
> That cleanliness, virtue and order reigned there.
> The tables and cupboards, which, opened to view,
> Shew'd the hand of industry had polished their hue.
> The shelves and their crockery, both china and delph,
> Were clean and were orderly rang'd on the shelf.
> Nor can we consent to call those people poor,
> Where prudence steps in, and bars want from the door

William Hutton, *Remarks upon North Wales*, 1803

'*A Dunghill modelld into the shape of a cottage ... it appeard not unlike a great blot of Cow-turd ... the light flowd in through the old circumference of a bottomless Peck (tub) being stuck in the Thatch ... The Door-way was a breach in the wall toward one end, which being of a dwarfish size ... we were forcd to abridge our Dimensions and to creep in ... We found no Apartments in these Habitations, every edifice being a Noahs Arc, where a Promiscuous Family, a Miscellaneous Heap of all kind of Creatures did converse together in one Room; the Pigs and the Pullen (poultry) and other Brutes either truckling under, or lying at the Bed's-feet*'

From W. Richards, *Wallography or the Britton Describ'd*, 1682

©NMW

Hendre'r-ywydd Uchaf was originally built in about 1508 at Llangynhafal, Denbighshire, and is now re-erected at St Fagans National History Museum (above). A single-storey farmstead with a floor hearthed hall, a bedchamber, and integral cow houses all under the same roof, this was a rather superior version of the 'cottages' which travellers described.

'A Dunghill modelld into the shape of a cottage ...' A romantic print (left) of a cottage on Kymin Hill, Monmouth, by Mannskirsch, dated 1799.

© National Library of Wales

Some Georgian observers noted that though many poorer Welsh country people still built and lived in one-room houses, these were more often divided into a living room and a *siambar* (bedchamber) by a timber partition or judiciously arranged furniture. Increasingly, too, cottages were being equipped with a *croglofft*, a half loft, usually reached by means of a ladder, which provided space for one or even two extra bedrooms. Householders with space to do so might loft over the whole ground floor to provide a complete upper storey.

Inside walls and timbers were generally limewashed in white, or colourwashed with either yellow ochre (which occurs naturally in parts of north-west Wales) or the red raddle also used for marking sheep. Treatment of the floor followed well established regional traditions. In Caernarvonshire, hard earthen floors were washed with sooty water, which after many applications made them shine. In south-west Wales, glazed floors were made using earth, lime, and sometimes bulls' blood. Elsewhere geometric patterns were marked out on the floor with white hearthstone or sand. In and around Montgomeryshire, floors in gentry houses as well as cottages and farmhouses were decoratively 'pitched' with stones set on edge, often arranged in complex designs.

Everywhere, textiles — in the form of bed curtains, quilts, and striped *carthen* blankets (the lineal descendants of the ancient *brychan* cloak-cum-coverlet) — added colour as well as warmth to cottage and farmhouse interiors. Well into the nineteenth century, such modest interiors perpetuated many long-standing Welsh decorative traditions, and remained (for the time being) quite independent of fashion.

© National Library of Wales

© National Library of Wales

© NMW

A painting of an interior at Tal-y-llyn, Gwynedd, in 1836 (above left), by E. P. Owen, shows the upper bedroom in the *croglofft* with its access ladder, and a cupboard-bed beside the fireplace. A Welsh dresser filled with display crockery stands prominently to the right.

A cottage interior at Harlech, Gwynedd, is shown in this watercolour of 1836, again by E. P. Owen (above). A huge Welsh dresser — incompletely painted — stands on the left, and to the right is a big wattle-and-daub fire hood, carrying off the smoke from what had perhaps been originally an open floor hearth.

The fire hood in Abernodwydd, a house from Llangadfan, Powys (left), which is now reconstructed at St Fagans National History Museum. Originally built in about 1678 as an open-hall farmhouse with a central floor hearth, in the early eighteenth century Abernodwydd was given this stone-backed fire hood rising to a timber-framed internal chimney. At the same time the whole house was lofted over to provide a complete upper storey.

The pitched floor at Tŷ Mawr, Llanwnnog, Powys (left), has an elaborate pattern. Notorious as dust traps, such floors were often later boarded over or replaced with machine-made tiles: but they can still be seen in several buildings around Llanidloes, including the Mount Inn (above).

At the Old Market Hall, Llanidloes, Powys (left), a reconstructed timber-framed wall, infilled with split laths and plastered, was colourwashed in yellow ochre.

Textiles added colour and pattern to even the humblest homes. These nineteenth-century striped *carthenni* (blankets) are woven in coarse wool and made from two narrow handloom widths joined side by side (below).

# Sham barons: Gothic fantasies

Among the multifarious nineteenth-century styles, the Gothic, or medieval revival, demands a section of its own, because it is so spectacularly represented in Wales. Sham castles, declared especially suitable for 'a bold or mountainous country', were in the early decades of the century already a passion among Welsh magnates, particularly those who had grown rich from the Industrial Revolution, which was simultaneously transforming the land.

In the north, the sprawling theatrical folly of Gwrych Castle, Conwy, was soon followed by Penrhyn Castle, near Bangor, built in 1820–37 for the slate-rich Pennants in the Norman revival style; and by Bodelwyddan Castle, Denbighshire, a Georgian mansion revamped in a castellated style by Joseph Hansom (inventor of the famous cab). In the south, copper-rich John Vivian built the neo-Tudor Singleton Abbey on the fringes of Swansea: and in 1824–25 the hard-headed Crawshay ironmasters built Cyfarthfa Castle — to a strict budget, and using rough stone hacked from the neighbouring hillside — to overlook their 'Pandaemonium of furnaces' in Merthyr Tydfil, the boom-town which was then the largest in Wales.

These sham castles, however, were only playing at being baronial residences. Their battlemented exteriors encased conventional late Georgian interiors with light touches of Gothic detail.

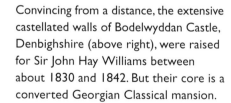

Set against a medieval-style ashlar-painted wall, this sham helmet of painted wood and plaster at Bodelwyddan Castle (above left) epitomizes the cosmetic baronial style of earlier Welsh castellated mansions.

Convincing from a distance, the extensive castellated walls of Bodelwyddan Castle, Denbighshire (above right), were raised for Sir John Hay Williams between about 1830 and 1842. But their core is a converted Georgian Classical mansion.

The battlemented fireplace (bottom left) in the Gothic entrance hall is one of the few interior features of Cyfarthfa Castle that even pretends to be medieval. The remainder of the interior is in the late Georgian Classical style.

Penrhyn Castle, Gwynedd (left), a rather more serious and archaeological exercise in medievalism, was by contrast purpose-built from the outset as an imitation castle. Designed by Thomas Hopper, it is the apogee of the neo-Norman style in Britain. Penrhyn's chief showpiece is its towering Norman-style keep. This lithograph (right) of its sumptously carved great hall, complete with early Victorian inhabitants, was made soon after its completion in 1837.

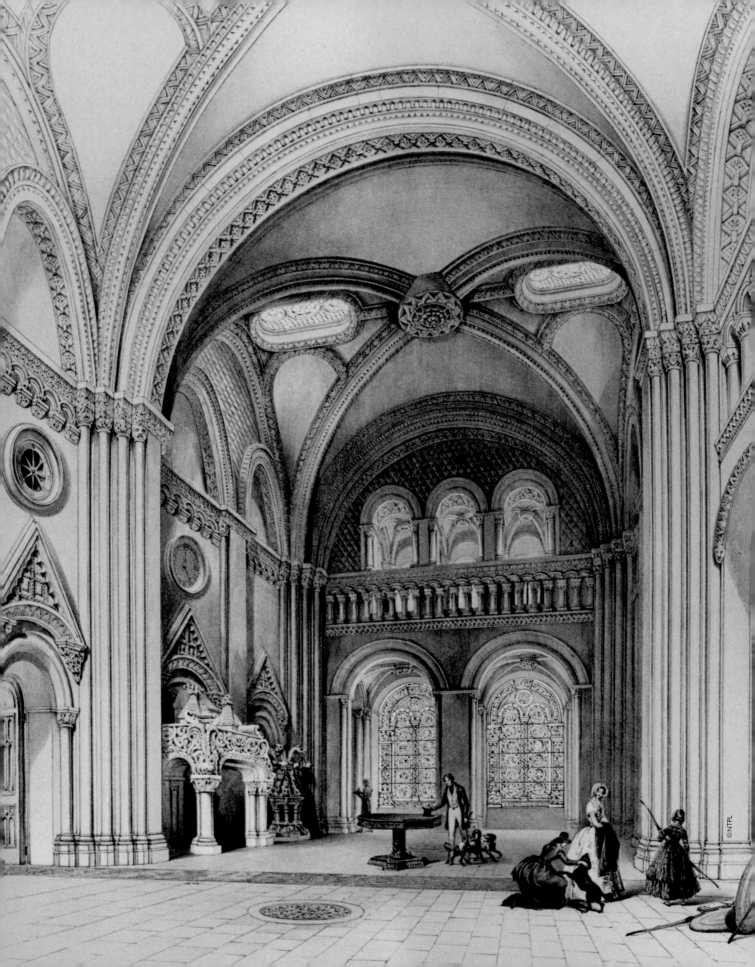

# Victorian to 'Modern'
# Interiors 1840–1960

# 'To Suit all Tastes and Pockets'

The period between 1840 and 1960, though the shortest in this book, was also the most eventful from two points of view. First, it saw the completion of the transformation of Wales from a largely rural to a largely industrial nation, with a population over four times greater in 1914 than it had been in 1770. Secondly, Wales changed from a land effectively ruled by aristocrats, squires and parsons to one dominated by industrialists, politicians, the chapel and the trades unions.

For Welsh and indeed British interiors also, this was an era of great change and almost bewildering variety. Queen Victoria's reign occupied half of the period, but there was no single Victorian style, nor even an orderly succession of Victorian styles. Rather, a whole series of decorative fashions were concurrently in vogue, often in rivalry with each other. Thus a prosperous householder of 1850 could choose for instance between 'Classical Grecian';

conservative 'Georgian survival'; 'medieval baronial'; or any permutation of these and other styles. Fifty years later, he might either choose the opulent, cluttered, and densely patterned interior now regarded as typically Victorian, or lean towards one of the many versions of the self-proclaimed 'pure and honest' Aesthetic style. Neither of course did Victorian styles disappear with the queen's death. Interiors almost indistinguishable from those of the 1870s could still be seen in some Welsh houses over a century later.

The most significant development in this period was to make an ever wider choice of decorating materials and styles available to an ever wider social range of householders. With the technological advances of the Victorian age, it was possible to produce infinitely cheaper wallpapers, mechanically roller printed rather than blocked by hand; cheaper machine-printed furnishing textiles, dyed with chemical dyes; and cheaper paints bought by the tin rather than mixed by the painter. Machine-cut veneers, machine-cut tiles, and even — to the distress of William Morris —

machine-cut wood-carving, all brought interior decorating prices tumbling down. So too did mass-produced Kidderminster or Brussels carpets, and later, the still cheaper, more durable, and more 'hygenic' linoleums.

At the peak of their popularity in the 1930s, more than one hundred million square yards of lino and similar floorings were sold in Britain in a single year: but three decades later these too had fallen victim to the even more rapid changes of the Plastics Age with which this survey ends. By then an immense variety of cheap, cheerful, and highly coloured decorating materials were accessible to all but the very poorest householder. The wording of a 1929 advertisement from the Royal Welsh Warehouse, Newtown, Powys, — 'Rooms to Suit All Tastes and Pockets' — could scarcely have become more true. There was however a disadvantage to this democratization of decoration. Since the same materials could be bought as easily in Rhyl or Newport or London or Leeds or Glasgow, interiors throughout Britain increasingly lost any remaining regional character.

The interiors of the Judge's Lodging at Presteigne, Powys, were fitted out during the 1840s–60s by the Radnorshire county magistrates. They had conservative tastes, and the rooms retain a distinctly Georgian air. In the recreated dining room (opposite), nearly all the oak furniture is original to the house. The red colour scheme was much favoured in Victorian times for eating rooms, as were candles for illumination. Though the servants' quarters at the Judge's Lodging were equipped with gas lighting in 1860, this was not considered socially acceptable above stairs.

The 'Georgian survival' colour scheme of this conservatively styled bedroom at the Judge's Lodging (above) was precisely recreated from surviving evidence.

The opposite extreme of Victorian style: Lord Bute's bedroom at Cardiff Castle (below) was fantastically — and extremely expensively — decorated in the Moorish Gothic style.

Somewhat cluttered but distinctly tasteful, this 1890s sitting room at Cefn Mably (above) displays 'scenic wallpaper'. Printed in highly coloured individual lengths which together made up a landscape or historical panorama, such papers were produced in France: fabulously expensive, they were affordable only by the fashionable rich.

More tasteful still: a fine example of the relatively uncluttered Aesthetic style is this room at Lester's Furnace Lodging (below), in about 1900. Among the carefully arranged ornaments are a small Pre-Raphaelite triptych and several Japanese-style fans, indispensable for Aesthetic decorators.

The entrance hall at Singleton Abbey, Swansea (right), is shown decorated in the medieval baronial style — complete with stuffed flamingo — in about 1895.

Victorian survival: this bedroom in Rhayader, Powys (far right) retained its original Victorian furnishings until the early 1990s.

The Arts and Crafts interior at its most 'honest', dignified and comfortable. The living room at High Glanau, Monmouthshire (below), built in 1922–23 as an 'amplified retirement cottage' for H. Avray Tipping, garden designer and architectural correspondent of *Country Life* magazine.

## Bute and Burges

By contrast with the sham castles of the early nineteenth century, Cardiff Castle and Castell Coch — the two extraordinary 'dream castles' built by the third marquess of Bute and his architect, William Burges — are something altogether different. Combining dedication to medieval ideals, exuberant imagination and limitless funds (since Bute was reputedly the richest man in the world), their fantasy interiors are the crowning glory of the Gothic Revival not only in Wales, but in all of Britain.

Castell Coch (above), a genuine but almost totally ruined medieval fortress 5 miles (8km) from Cardiff, was 'restored' between 1875 and 1891 as an occasional summer residence. Despite their efforts to seek authentic medieval precedents in Britain, Bute and Burges created a fairy-tale castle in the woods, with distinctive conical roofs more reminiscent of France or Switzerland.

No medieval home was complete without its banqueting hall. At Cardiff Castle (above right), Burges created this huge and magnificent hall by demolishing the seven bedrooms which previously occupied its site. The most seriously antiquarian of the castle's rooms, its decoration celebrates the deeds of Robert, earl of Gloucester, builder of the nearby twelfth-century keep, and those of Lord Bute's own Scottish ancestors.

The Winter Smoking Room at Cardiff Castle is shown (below left) in a watercolour of 1870 by Axel Herman Haig, and (below) as it was completed in 1872 and still remains. All the sumptuous Bute and Burges rooms have decorative themes; in this case it is 'Time and the Seasons'. The concept of a medieval smoking room, equipped with a buffet containing drawers for cigars, may be thought absurd, but is typical of the eccentricity of Victorian High Gothic.

In the less public rooms of Cardiff Castle, Burges did not allow his exuberant imagination to be restrained by British or even European medieval sources. The Arab Room (right), in the Moorish Gothic style, has a gilded stalactite ceiling. At Cardiff Castle and at Castell Coch, the alliance between the pious, reclusive and studious Lord Bute, and his quirkier, worldlier and more irreverent architect/decorator produced unforgettable results.

The country interiors of Castell Coch are rather lighter in feeling than those of ceremonious Cardiff Castle, but equally crowded with layer upon layer of symbolism. The rib-vaulted ceiling of the drawing room (right) is thronged with birds, an element of the room's theme: 'Life and Death in Nature'.

The decorative schemes of both castles — which were rarely occupied, as the Butes spent more time in Scotland and London or abroad than in Wales — have survived in remarkably original condition. In both places the furnishings are being refurbished. Lord Bute's copper-plated cast-iron bed with crystal finials has been recently restored and replaced in his bedchamber at Castell Coch (below).

In Lady Bute's domed bedchamber at Castell Coch (left), the main decorative theme is 'the Sleeping Beauty'. It contains an astounding Gothic castellated wash stand, with tanks for hot and cold water in its turrets.

The cheerful day nursery at Cardiff Castle (above) displays a Burges tiled frieze with a procession of characters from fables and fairy tales, including 'the Invisible Prince' (who appears only in outline). The chimney piece

has the more moralistic theme of 'Good- and Ill-Fame'.

Every detail of the furnishing of both castles had to be approved by the marquess of Bute and his wife, Lady Gwendolen.

# A photograph album of Welsh interiors 1885–1925

Photography, developed near the beginning of Victoria's reign, has added to our knowledge of interiors of this period — but rather less than might be hoped. For room interiors were not easy to photograph without complicated lighting, so early photographers naturally much preferred outdoor scenes. When photographs of interiors become more numerous, from the 1880s, they nearly always depict the rooms of the wealthy. Pictures of middle- and working-class homes are not common, and photographs of the poorest Welsh houses are extremely rare.

This photograph of about 1885 (top left) was taken by the self-taught Welsh photographer, John Thomas, who for forty years travelled all over Wales recording scenes and people for his Cambrian Gallery. One of his few interior views, it shows the crowded furnishings of the drawing room at Coed-coch, a Georgian mansion in Betws-yn-Rhos, Denbighshire. The fine painted panelling is Georgian, but the chairs with their chintz loose covers

were perhaps fairly new when the photograph was taken.

Photographed forty years later in about 1925, the less cluttered drawing room at Cottrell (above left), could well be late Victorian, save that the candles seem to be wired for electricity and a photograph of a soldier in World War I uniform stands on the table in the foreground. The wall coverings could be fine wallpaper, or perhaps silk damask.

A large neo-Classical mansion 5 miles (8km) from Cowbridge, Vale of Glamorgan, Cottrell was empty after 1941 and demolished in 1970.

Though known as the 'Haunted Bedroom', this room at Cefn Mably (above right), looks a comparatively cheerful place in June 1895. The bed has a head cloth and half canopy, perhaps in cotton, and the wallpaper looks like a product of the William Morris workshop.

The Chinese Bedroom at Singleton Abbey (right), was photographed in 1894. Despite the Chinese-style wallpaper and other surface embellishments, the curtained four-poster bed makes the room appear more medieval. Singleton Abbey was a neo-Tudor mansion of the late 1820s, built for the Swansea copper-smelting magnate John Henry Vivian: it is now the administrative headquarters of the University of Wales Swansea.

A collection of antiquities in a country house was the hallmark both of scholarship and real or imaginary noble lineage. This is Dr Thomas's Oak Room at Gloddaeth, near Llandudno (below), photographed in about 1900.

© Archives, Swansea University

©RCAHMW

Gwydyr Castle, Drawing Room.

In the cavernous drawing room of Gwydir Castle (top left), seen here in a touched-up postcard of about 1900, there was no need to imitate antiquity. From plastered ceiling to tapestries and panelling, nearly all its decoration was entirely genuine.

A rare photograph of a middle-class interior of the very early twentieth century (middle left). Though described as a kitchen, this room at Maesyrychain, Llangollen, clearly also served as a living room. It is quite fashionably decorated, with an Art Nouveau-style border to the wallpaper and lustre ware on the mantelpiece. There are also photographs of ministers and a full case of weighty looking books. The family members clustered round the chenille-covered table are the epitome of studiousness, and are obviously wearing their best clothes: did they don them for the photographer, or had they perhaps just returned from chapel?

The family of the railway carter William Cooke of Morriston, Swansea, photographed not long before World War I (bottom left). The woman in the foreground may be a servant, a sign that the family had taken the recognized first step towards middle-class gentility. The view shows the floral wallpaper, and what seems to be a slatted window screen. The family look distinctly less composed — or posed — than their Llangollen counterparts, and the skimpiness of the tea-table cloth may indicate that this photograph was not so carefully set up.

# Country interiors

From 1840, the population of rural Wales went into steep and seemingly irreversible decline, as workers were drawn to the industrial regions of the nation or forced into emigration by a succession of agricultural depressions. Welsh rural dwellings — described, painted and later photographed as quaint survivals during the later nineteenth and early twentieth centuries — were thus increasingly endangered. They eventually came to be recognized as irreplaceable treasure houses of national and regional folk culture, including traditional interior decoration. In the decades following World War II, some threatened examples were saved and reconstructed at the pioneering Welsh Folk Museum (now known as St Fagans National History Museum).

The ever dwindling number of people who lived in working farmhouses and rural cottages, however, could not be expected to maintain them merely as picturesque museum pieces. They too adopted the new cheaper and more convenient decorating materials and technologies. Home-produced and locally made textiles were among the last surviving elements of urban as well as rural interiors which were distinctively Welsh. But even these were subject to twentieth-century technological developments and changes of fashion.

The timber-framed farmhouse, Abernodwydd, from Llangadfan, Powys (right), was built in about 1678 by Rhys Evan, and was still occupied by his probable descendants when this photograph was taken in about 1900.

By the 1950s, the farmhouse was abandoned and derelict, its thatch covered with corrugated iron (far right) — a new material embraced with enthusiasm by rural householders — and its framing panels bricked up or boarded over. In 1955 it was re-erected at the newly created Welsh Folk Museum, now St Fagans National History Museum.

Significantly entitled simply *In Wales*, this cottage interior was painted by Richard Ansdell in about 1840 (below right), probably in Snowdonia. A favourite with Victorian tourists and artists, picturesque stone-built and whitewashed Snowdonian cottages were then wrongly regarded as typically Welsh. Only much later were other regional traditions of building, furnishing and decoration widely recognized.

A Snowdonian quarryman's cottage of whitewashed boulders, Llainfadyn, from Rhostryfan, near Caernarfon (right), was built in 1762 and re-erected at St Fagans National History Museum exactly two centuries later. It is here shown with interior furnishings of about 1870. Their good quality illustrates the relatively high pay of quarrymen.

The interior of Cilewent in the Elan Valley, Powys, in 1954 (below), when it was still a working farm. Attended by china dogs, the radio has pride of place on a mirror-topped Victorian sideboard. A traditional longhouse with integral cow houses — glimpsed in the background — Cilewent was begun in the fifteenth century and rebuilt in 1734. A year after this picture was taken the house was superseded by a modern bungalow, and it now stands in St Fagans National History Museum.

Old and new interior decoration at Tynygerddi, near Llanfair Caereinion, Powys (above centre), perhaps during the late 1970s. The motif-incised beam across the timber-framed fire hood probably dates from the late seventeenth or early eighteenth century, when this style of timber adornment was popular in Montgomeryshire houses. The bottom layer of wallpaper which covers the close-studded timber-framed wall seems to be Victorian, the upper layer perhaps a little later. The floor covering is red quarry tiles, a cheap and practical successor to an earthen or pitched-stone floor.

Living with a historic fireplace at Hafoty, Anglesey (above right), before the house was restored by Cadw. The massive early Tudor hall fireplace (see p. 28) has been partly bricked up to accommodate a smaller and more practical fire grate, whose heat is reflected by a silver paper coating. Silver paper was also often used to damp-proof walls, generally with disastrous long-term results.

The Victorian wallpaper here seems to have suffered from damp: it covers an original stone wall, not an ideal surface for wallpaper.

The interiors of some prosperous farmhouses, especially near towns, differed little from those of middle-class urban houses. This is the comfortable gas-lit parlour at Llwyn-yr-Eos (opposite), a tenant farm on the St Fagans estate near Cardiff, recreated as it might have appeared during the 1930s.

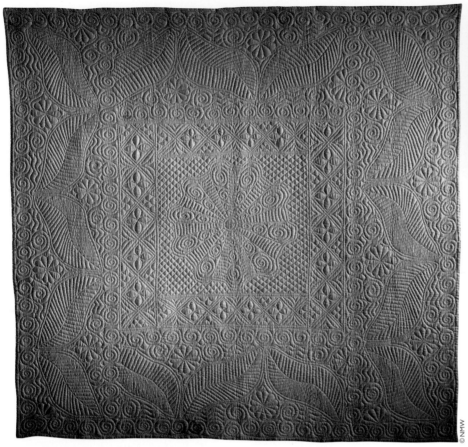

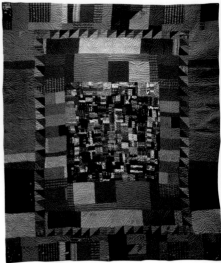

Home-made quilts were favoured in Wales longer than in many parts of Britain. They might be 'wholecloth' quilts with elaborate quilting patterns (above left), like this example made by Mary Morgans for her brother, Stephen, in 1905: or the better-known and more striking patchwork quilts (above), like this one made in Carmarthenshire in about 1860–70. After World War I, however, home-made quilts increasingly lost ground to mass-produced eiderdowns, satin-effect quilts, and candlewick bedspreads.

The *carthen* blanket continued to be woven in small west Wales mills as late as the 1950s, though many twentieth-century examples (left) used yarns dyed with chemicals. These modern colours were less subtle than the earlier hues obtained from vegetable dyes. Coverlets and other furnishings of reversible 'Welsh Tapestry' — as seen here (far left) on the old-fashioned curtained bed of Mrs Laura Pritchard, Clogwyn Bach, Penygroes, in the 1960s — remained popular longest of all, and are still produced.

# The interiors of workers' houses

By far the largest number of older houses in Wales today were built for industrial or other urban workers, the great majority of them in the south and south-east of the country. By 1851 two-thirds of the people of Wales lived in these areas.

By 1914 nearly half of them were concentrated in the industrial areas of south-east Wales alone, in areas which, until the iron and coal boom scarcely a century and a half earlier, had been virtually unpeopled uplands. Thus the small rural village of Merthyr Tydfil mushroomed during the single generation before 1801 into the largest town in Wales; the population of the coalfield parish of Bedwellte increased by 1,795 per cent between 1801 and 1851; and that of Aberdare more than doubled in the single decade between 1851 and 1861.

Little is known about the interior decoration of the industrial boom-town dwellings which housed the first tidal waves of Welsh, Irish and English immigrants. Lacking the romantic appeal of country cottages, their interiors were very rarely painted or photographed: descriptions of them by crusading reformers understandably concentrated on their sometimes appallingly insanitary and overcrowded squalor, rather than the efforts which some householders undoubtedly made to brighten their surroundings.

From the 1870s onwards, due to new and long-overdue housing regulations, the most squalid of the earlier dwellings were swept away, and replaced with better-planned, better-built and more comfortable terraced housing. The upsurge of coalfield prosperity in the early twentieth century, and the availability of mass-produced materials, also allowed more ambitious interior decoration in urban houses.

After the traumas of the Depression and World War II, the late 1940s and 1950s saw a new wave of both house building and house decoration. Much of this was concentrated in working-class areas. Eighty-seven per cent of dwellings built in Wales between 1947 and 1951 were council houses. These included tens of thousands of well-designed prefabricated aluminium bungalows, or 'prefabs'.

During the post-war years before 1960, improved housing, an apparently more secure economic future, and above all an ever widening range of inexpensive and easily available materials all combined to provoke an unprecedented boom in 'do-it-yourself' home improvements. Interior decoration had arrived for all the people of Wales.

This unidentified barrack dwelling in mid-Wales exemplifies the most basic type of temporary housing for the single labourers who provided muscle for the new industries throughout the nineteenth century. It was photographed in about 1901, and newspapers depicting the Boer War can be seen used as wallpaper. Four men shared the two beds, cooking their meals on the grate and eating them on the table to the right.

© NMW

The new industries desperately needed skilled and experienced workmen as well as manual labourers, so industrialists needed to build housing to attract and retain them and their families. The terrace from Rhyd-y-car was constructed in about 1800 by the Crawshays for their valued Merthyr Tydfil ironstone miners. It has been reconstructed at St Fagans National History Museum. This interior recreates a respectable working family's home of about 1855 (top left).

A typical room of 1925 in the same row (top right). The walls are papered, and there are many more ornaments and home comforts on display.

A reconstructed child's bedroom of about 1950 (middle left) in a prefab from Gabalfa, Cardiff, now at St Fagans National History Museum. Many prefabs were equipped not only with two bedrooms and a living room, but also a fitted kitchen (middle right) with a cooker and a refrigerator, and a fitted bathroom with a heated towel rail. These were luxuries previously unattainable for many working householders, and the prefab was hailed as a housewife's paradise.

Inhabitants of older houses also demanded more space and better facilities in the post-war era. This reconstructed 'living room shed' of about 1955 (opposite), was built in the garden of a house in the terrace from Rhyd-y-car. It allowed the original parlour within the house (left) to be used as a best sitting room or 'television lounge'.

# Gazetteer and map of important buildings

1 **Abernodwydd** Llangadfan, Powys E3, pp. 66, 81

2 **Althrey Hall** Bangor Iscoed, Flintshire F2, p. 36

3 **Bachegraig** Denbigh, Denbighshire E1, p. 23

4 **Bachymbyd Fawr** Vale of Clwyd, Denbighshire E2, pp. 40, 45

5 **Bodelwyddan** nr Abergele, Denbighshire E1, p. 68

6 **Caerau** Llanfair-yng-Nghornwy, Anglesey C1, p. 39

7 **Caernarfon Castle** Gwynedd C2, pp. 7, 11

8 **Caerphilly Castle** Caerphilly E6, pp. 11, 12, 13

9 **Cardiff Castle** Cardiff E7, pp. 72, 74, 75, 77

10 **Carew Castle** Pembrokeshire B6, pp. 23, 24, 27, 37, 38

11 **Castell Coch** Cardiff E7, pp. 74, 76, 77

12 **Castell Dinas Brân** nr Llangollen, Denbighshire E2, pp. 10, 11

13 **Castellymynach** Creigiau, Cardiff E7, p. 36

14 **Castell y Bere** nr Tywyn, Gwynedd D3, p. 14

15 **Cefn Mably** nr Cardiff E7, pp. 32, 72, 78

16 **Chepstow Castle** Monmouthshire F6, pp. 11, 12, 14, 17, 19, 25, 63

17 **Chirk Castle** Wrexham F2, pp. 27, 48, 50, 53

18 **Cilewent** Elan Valley, Powys E4, p. 82

19 **Cochwillan** Bethesda, Gwynedd D1, pp. 26, 30, 31

20 **Coed-coch** Betws-yn-Rhos, Denbighshire D1, p. 78

21 **Cold Knap Farm** Barry, Vale of Glamorgan E7, p. 36

22 **Conwy Castle** Conwy D1, pp. 11, 12, 21

23 **Cottrell** Cowbridge, Vale of Glamorgan E7, p. 78

24 **Cyfarthfa Castle** Merthyr Tydfil E6, p. 68

25 **Denbigh Castle** Denbighshire E2, pp. 15, 45

26 **Dinas Powys Hill Fort** Dinas Powys, Vale of Glamorgan E7, p. 5

27 **Dolforwyn Castle** nr Newtown, Powys E4, p. 8

28 **Egryn** Llanaber, Gwynedd C3, p. 32

29 **Elwy Bank** St Asaph, Denbighshire E1, p. 64

30 **Emral Hall** Worthenbury, Flintshire F2, p. 44

31 **Erddig** Wrexham F2, pp. 50, 51

32 **Far Hall** Llanddewi Ystradenni, Powys E4, p. 29

33 **Fonmon Castle** Barry, Vale of Glamorgan E7, pp. 48, 49, 51, 53, 57

34 **Prefab** Gabalfa, Cardiff E7 p. 86

35 **Gloddaeth** Llandudno, Conwy D1, pp. 23, 26, 28, 31, 34, 45, 79

36 **Great Castle House** Monmouth, Monmouthshire F6, pp. 46, 47, 52, 54

37 **Gwrych Castle** nr Abergele, Conwy D1, p. 68

38 **Gwydir Castle** nr Llanrwst, Conwy D2, pp. 23, 24, 41, 45, 58, 80

39 **Hafoty** nr Llanddona, Anglesey C1, pp. 28, 82

40 **Harlech Castle** Gwynedd C3, p. 7

41 **Hendre'r-ywydd Uchaf** Llangynhafal, Denbighshire E2, p. 65

42 **Kennixton Farmhouse** Llangynydd, Swansea C6, p. 38

43 **King's Head** Monmouth, Monmouthshire F6, pp. 54, 55

44 **Lamphey Bishop's Palace** Pembrokeshire B6, pp. 19, 23, 37, 38

45 **Llainfadyn** Rhostryfan, nr Caernarfon, Gwynedd C2, p. 82

46 **Llangedwyn** Powys E3, pp. 58, 60

47 **Llangorse Lake** East of Brecon, Powys E6, p. 5

48 **Llanvihangel Court** Abergavenny, Monmouthshire F6, pp. 40, 41, 44, 49

49 **Llanynys Church** Ruthin, Denbighshire E2, p. 40

50 **Llwyn-yr-Eos** St Fagans, Cardiff E7, pp. 82, 83

51 **Maenan Hall** Llanrwst, Conwy D2, p. 44

52 **Mount Inn** Llanidloes, Powys E4, p. 67

53 **Nant Wallter** Taliaris, Carmarthenshire D5, p. 48

54 **Nantclwyd House** Ruthin, Denbighshire E2, p. 30

55 **Nanteos** nr Aberystwyth, Ceredigion D4, p. 48

56 **Old Gwernyfed** Felindre, Hay-on-Wye, Powys E5, p. 41

57 **Old Impton** Presteigne, Powys F4, p. 30

58 **Old Market Hall** Llanidloes, Powys E4, pp. 34, 35, 67

59 **Oxwich Castle** Swansea C7, pp. 23, 27

60 **Partrishow (Patricio) Church** nr Abergavenny, Powys E6, p. 30

61 **Pembroke Castle** Pembrokeshire B6, pp. 19, 21

62 **Penarth** Newtown, Powys E4, p. 24

63 **Penarth Fawr** nr Pwllheli, Gwynedd C2, pp. 28, 30, 45

64 **Penrhyn Castle** Bangor, Gwynedd D1, p. 68

65 **Pibwrlwyd** Llangunnor, Carmarthenshire C6, p. 61

66 **Picton Castle** Haverfordwest, Pembrokeshire B6, pp. 48, 50, 51, 53, 56, 58

67 **Plasau Duon** Clatter, Powys E4, p. 24

68 **Plas Dolben** Llangynhafal, Denbighshire E2, p. 32

69 **Plas Mawr** Conwy D1, pp. 3, 23, 24, 25, 26, 29, 38, 43, 44, 58, 59

70 **Plas Mawr** Caernarfon, Gwynedd C2, p. 48

71 **Plas Teg** Hope, Flintshire F2, pp. 23, 24

72 **Portmeirion** nr Pwllheli, Gwynedd C2, p. 44

73 **Powis Castle** Welshpool, Powys E3, pp. 27, 41, 48

74 **Raglan Castle** Monmouthshire F6, pp. 22, 23, 24, 25, 27, 29, 37, 47, 52

75 **Rhosyr** Newbrough, Anglesey C2, pp. 5, 7

76 **Rhuddlan Castle** Denbighshire E1, p. 18

77 **Rhyd-y-car** Merthyr Tydfil E6, pp. 86, 87

78 **St Davids Bishop's Palace** Pembrokeshire A5, pp. 15, 21

79 **St Fagans Castle** Cardiff E7, p. 27

80 **Singleton Abbey** Swansea D6, pp. 68, 73, 79

81 **Skenfrith Castle** Monmouthshire F6, p. 12

82 **Strata Florida** Old House, Ceredigion D4, p. 6

83 **The Judge's Lodging** Presteigne, Powys F4 pp. 61, 70, 71

84 **Tredegar House** Newport F7, pp. 47, 54

85 **Tretower Court** nr Crickhowell, Powys E6, pp. 23, 33

86 **Tynygerddi** Llanfair Caereinion, Powys E3, p. 82

87 **Upper Dolley** Ackhill, nr Presteigne, Powys E4, p. 39

88 **Upper House** Discoed, Powys E4, pp. 24, 36

89 **Upper House** Painscastle, Powys E5, p. 63

90 **Weobley Castle** Llanrhidian, Swansea C6, pp. 15, 23

91 **Wynnstay** formerly Wattstay, Ruabon, Wrexham F2, p. 58